'An evocative book ... I could taste the salt on my lips and smell the perfume of storm petrels. *The Seafarers* is a pelagic poem about the birds that exist at the coastal edges of our islands and consciousness. The stories of these hardy birds entwine seamlessly with Stephen Rutt's personal journey to form a narrative as natural and flowing as the passage of shearwater along the face of Atlantic rollers.'
– Jon Dunn, author of *Orchid Summer*

'A beautifully illuminating portrait of lives lived largely on the wing and at sea ... In this intimate guide to the wild beauty and complexity of seabirds, Stephen Rutt has written a powerful chronicle of resilience and fragility.'
– Julian Hoffman, author of *Irreplaceable* and *The Small Heart of Things*

WINTERING

A Season With Geese

Stephen Rutt

Elliott&Thompson

First published 2019 by
Elliott and Thompson Limited
2 John Street, London WC1N 2ES
www.eandtbooks.com

This paperback edition first published in 2020

ISBN: 978-1-78396-505-2

9 8 7 6 5 4 3 2 1

A catalogue record for this book is available from the British Library.

Cover design by Dan Mogford
Typesetting by Marie Doherty
Printed and bound by CPI Group (UK) Ltd, Croydin CR0 4YY

For my parents

Contents

Introduction

Autumn begins as a season for movement, and ends with everything changed.

From the boggy pools of the Scandinavian taiga forests, west to the far coast of Greenland and east to the Arctic coast of Siberia, geese are breeding. Throughout the far north, birds have been raising young all summer long, making the most of the season of light and food. From the cliffs of Svalbard, where they have been breeding out of paw reach of polar bears, barnacle geese goslings have jumped before they are capable of flying, landing in the soft embrace of Arctic tundra. The fortunate will make it. In the volcanic central plateau of Iceland, pink-footed geese have survived a season of being strafed by eagles and battered by the capricious Icelandic climate. These geese of the north are converting food into yellow fat, stored just beneath their skin, ready to fuel the long flight in a skein pointing south. Five wild species will head to Britain for the winter: a relative land of plenty, and gentler weather, respite from a north that is, still, ice-blasted and snowbound for the winter.

Mid-September in southern England. A long hot summer is slowly burning up. The grass is parched. We drive north into our new life.

And I am not interested in geese yet.

Some interests can't be explained. But they can perhaps be rationalised. My favourite writer on birds, J. A. Baker, wrote, 'I came late to the love of birds.'[1] I can't say that – I've been birding for almost half my life now – but I did come late to the love of geese. Their habit of always just being there, their familiarity, bred apathy.

I knew two sorts. The grey-brown geese of park lakes, eating bread, arguing noisily with each other, with anything. And I knew the wild geese, the grey and black ones, the migratory species that are another cog in the supposedly seamless cycle in the seasons of the northern hemisphere. I wasn't that interested. Growing up in East Anglia introduced me to a wild wealth of birds – geese were just one small blip on my personal radar, calibrated more to the waders and the warblers. There was no reason to look at geese. They were always just there.

Sometimes it takes another person to tell you something about yourself that should have been obvious. It was early in our relationship that Miranda said I was obsessed with the seasons. Registering them, tracking the changes: the arrivals and the blooming, the departures and the dying. I had never really thought about why, but with the clarity of hindsight it seems to make sense. The year we met was the year that I called four different places home. Then six places in four years. Perhaps I saw the seasons as something to anchor myself by, in the absence of putting down real roots in one place or in one long-term rented house. Perhaps I saw, without knowing, the seasons as a constant in my own period of upheaval.

The sixth home was a big move – the biggest, the most permanent that we had done together. Three hundred and fifty miles north and west by road, a seven-hour journey with our cat in a carrier. My partner, Miranda, was leaving to study for a PhD and I was following with trepidation. All I had to do was finish a book. I had no job to transfer seamlessly into, and not much in the way of savings either. We were moving out of Essex and into Dumfries, a little town tucked away in the corner of Scotland, barely beyond the English border. Dumfries was perched on the edge of the estuary hinterland: flat, green and exceptionally muddy. It felt familiar. In the other direction, the entirely unfamiliar: hills and pine trees; moors studded with wind turbines.

⌣

We arrive in a gale, just before the decaying of chlorophyll turns the tree leaves from green to gold, into an empty flat on the edge of town. It smells musty. The aroma of the previous occupant's cigarettes has burrowed deep into the paisley carpet and the floral curtains. She had spent almost all of her ninety-seven years in this flat and her presence is stronger than just the smell: it feels as if we're visitors in someone else's home. Our cat is silent. She has miaowed herself hoarse on the journey up and is stalking around suspiciously at the lack of objects to hide behind. Until the boxes arrive.

The first full day is relentless. The flat is overflowing with boxes and electricians and the men who come to sort the internet. Our visitors warn us that the gale has become a storm. That the traffic lights at the end of the road are out. That street signs are swaying. That trees are falling all around us and that I should retrieve the neighbour's wheelie bin that has landed in our garden, plastic sacks strewn across our lawn. In exchange, a box blows open and my shirts greet the gnomes in the neighbour's garden. The sill blows off our bedroom window. Cormorants fly up the river and past us as if they are arrows, shot by the breeze. From the kitchen window we can see someone else's polytunnel, the polythene at first frayed and flapping and then flying off.

Evening draws the sting from the storm. Our windows look west, to where the light cracks through the clouds and spills brightly behind the hills. The yellow light warms the rows of grey pebble-dash terraces that are stacked back towards the rugby pitches on the edge of town. We have two lines of hills. A low one, which peaks just above the rooftiles and aerials, with a black line of trees. Behind them:

bigger hills, thicker woods, a texture to a landscape that the flatness of Essex has not prepared me for. The way light lends contrast to hillsides, picks out some in glorious burning brightness and shades in others. The chiaroscuro after the storm.

It was a week before we gave ourselves the freedom to have fun. The decorating done, the shed door reattached, bookcases reassembled and our books out of their boxes and into some sort of order. We go for a walk, following a path looping up around the far edge of town, in the rich warming light of the midday sun. It illuminates the remaining chaos of the storm. Great boughs of plane trees have broken, pushed and pulled from their trunks by the eddying wind and lie, split, next to the path. Others are wedged in the river, like the work of the beavers that would once have been here. Some block the path entirely and we scramble over them. It feels good to be outside after the stresses of moving house. It feels good to be here before the leaves turn, so we can begin with the beginning of autumn.

The decision to come feels worth it. In the sunshine a buzzard leaps out of a tree on the other side of the river. It cries twice, spirals overhead, then lifts up, soaring high on open wings, as if carrying our stresses with it. I feel eager for the autumn. Birds punctuate my year: time passes constantly but birds are the grammar of its passing, they give a rough working order to the months. I have my totems: the first singing chiffchaff at the beginning of spring and the first screeching swift at its end. The silencing of song at the end of summer; the disappearance of the swifts and the arrivals of autumn. The extra thrushes: the redwings gently whistling through the autumn night and the fieldfares clattering along fruit-laden hedgerows.

And now I have a new totem. By the time we get home from our walk the light is thick and golden, descending over the western hills. We make ourselves tea and watch the sky turn, anticipating the colour of the leaves to come. And that's when we see the first skein. A simple arrow of birds as distant as the hills, heading south through the sunset. It is 23 September. Our winter of geese about to begin.

1

Pink-footed Geese

Tedious chores. Another week passes with the organising of bills, the sorting of paperwork: the knitting together of stuff that makes a new home, a new life. I take a council tax form to the council offices. On my way out I take a short cut through the car park towards the library. It takes a second or two when you're somewhere unfamiliar for something to make sense. I know the sound – the sound of pink-footed geese. I do not know it in this context: one bare tree, hundreds of parked cars, buildings behind me and to both sides. I stand, dumbfounded for a few seconds, confused by my ears and staring at a blank sky, the only movement the steady drift of clouds. Then, as if detaching from the bare branches of the tree, a skein of geese appears behind it, low in the sky. A large chevron. Uneven, roughly three times longer on the left-hand side than the right. Less like a skein, more like a contour drifting off the map from the hills to the north, floating noisily over town. I take a few photos on my phone as they pass behind the spire of a church. I count them in the waiting room of the GP's surgery. Each goose a black speck against grey. A hundred and twenty black specks.

Our winter of geese. My winter of wild half-count, half-estimates at the numbers passing overhead, between the fields north of the town and the Solway Firth to the south. Miranda's winter of saying, 'Ssssh! Can you hear the geese?' and counting skeins on her walk to and from the university.

Dumfries and the Solway Firth's winter of geese. It is the same across Scotland, the Lancashire mosses, the Dyfi and the Severn, and the low mud estuaries of eastern England, and lasts for the true length of winter: from late September until early April. The pink-footed goose's winter: a thousand-mile flight from Iceland and then a seamless swap from summer to winter. I envy its lack of paperwork.

September slips into October. I could still go out without a coat. Watch the trees on the distant hill turn ochre, bronze and gold. And the geese were never far away. More exploratory walks: along both banks of the river, north and south. Both would turn up geese. Sitting at my desk finishing my book, I would look up and out of the window and see geese swirling around the fields on the edge of town, at the height of the television aerials of the next terrace, like visible static. I couldn't decide if they were taunting me or helping me. Taunting me: deskbound and unable to give myself the time away from my book to walk to the edge of the estate, find them and watch them. Or helping me: giving me a brief flash of the wild outside in an otherwise housebound day. I would hear their calls first. A high-pitched squeak. An abbreviated *wink wink* repeated en masse, each individual call blurring into others.

I have lived enough in single-glazed southern houses, where the windows didn't properly fit the frame, where the gap under the front door allowed light and draught and sound in from the outside. Hearing the starlings singing or snatches of conversation from the street in my living room was normal. It is not so here in this Scottish flat. It is sturdily built, and everything fits flush and double glazing gives us the blessing of insulation. It is not that I particularly desire to be shut off from the outside world – I just don't want to be cold any more. The trade-off is a dulling of the birdsong. The discovery is that geese calls bleed through the walls and windows anyway. That is joyous.

It is our winter of running to the windows as they pass over.

Now I am interested in geese.

I am falling more deeply for geese on a daily basis. Although I am told the winter won't always be like this – they are wild geese after all, predictably unpredictable – the regular skeins flying over are captivating me. Sinking deep inside me. It is new for me. In a new place they are making me feel, tentatively, at home. Connected to the world, while it just happens around me, daily and unadorned. It is not a famous spectacle, these passing skeins of geese, not the top billing on wildlife TV. These geese just quietly go about their daily movements, as I go about mine. I am one insignificant human to them but they are reminding me that I am a part of the world that stretches as far away as Iceland, part of the running rhythm of winter.

The British winter begins with the arrival of five species: the barnacle, the brent, the bean, the white-fronted and the pink-footed. All bar the barnacle and the pink-footed come in different, discernible forms depending on where they have come from. Despite this there are some essential similarities to all these geese. They all breed in the far, far north: Greenland, Franz Josef Land, Arctic Siberia, Iceland, Svalbard, Scandinavia. Geese are faithful to places; their needs are unique.

Geese are herbivores, like avian cattle, but they need the right length and sort of grassland. Each species has a bill tailored for what they eat: a short bill for picking up plants between the blades of grass or a bigger bill for digging out the rhizomes under the soil surface. How they use their bill differs too. Barnacle geese can peck 230 times a minute, a frantic sewing-machine-like feeding, that will comprise most of their daily activity – and with a bright moon a decent part of the night as well.[1] Their digestive systems are inefficient – most of what goes into a goose comes out of a goose pretty much as it went in – but geese have developed efficient strategies to help them overcome this problem. Brent geese, for example, focus their feeding on the top part of the grass, then return several days later to the same patch, when the grazed grass has grown back at twice the usual rate and the nutrients are packed into the new growth. Undigested goose droppings help fertilise the Arctic soil, promoting further grass growth, while the droppings also provide a source of food for reindeer. Reindeer and cattle have a much slower digestion, enabling them to extract much more nutrition from their diet than geese can. That's why geese have to constantly eat the best-quality food they can. If there are geese in a field, it has good grass.

Geese also need a place away from predators to spend the night. Estuaries and marshes and vast harvested fields suit them. Once they find a place, they tend to return, instead of seeking out somewhere new. Home for geese is cold but comfortable and familiar and seasonal, twice yearly. It is safer for them to be this way. Once they find their homes, they tend not to move from them.

These pink-footed geese know Dumfries better than we do. The skeins we see scoring the sky are following regular routes. Well-travelled sky paths. Geese can be long-lived, if they avoid foxes, polar bears, power lines and men with guns: the average life expectancy is eight years, but the oldest recorded bird was thirty-eight when it died. The Solway has seen pink-feet live through to their twenties. These are just the ringed birds that we know about, that have been found again. In the thousand-strong flocks there could be some that are older. I wonder at the generations of geese contained in each skein.

A morning, a week later. The first skein comes, shaped like the nib of a fountain pen, drawing a northbound line through the sky. I am walking northeast through the town, to the station, on an early golden morning. The third skein skips across, between the roofs of the shops, just off the high street. The fifth veers off eastward, into the sun. The sixth is the vanguard of the two-coach rattling train to Glasgow, ploughing its slow way through the hills to the city.

I look up the word 'skein' on slow mobile internet from the train. It's from the old, obscure French word 'escaigne', meaning an amount of yarn. The word makes a sort of sense. Although it is the only use of the word 'skein' that does not have a textile meaning, I like the way it suggests threads. Threads of geese in the sky, sometimes unravelling, sometimes like a ball of string, trailing a loose end. The skeins we see are stringy strands of the geese. It is only roughly, only occasionally, the precise V-shape of the classic imagined geese skein. Each flock is social. It seems mildly ironic that we should move to a place where I know nobody, and for the birds to be obviously together, benefiting each other. These skeins are social forms of flying. Each goose reduces drag for the one behind it. Each goose helps another.

It is possible to think these skeins ancient, that they have been scoring the sky since time beyond memory. It's not true. British pink-footed geese come almost entirely from Iceland and Greenland. The rest of Europe's come from Svalbard, the archipelago halfway between Norway and the North Pole. The Icelandic population increased spectacularly during the twentieth century. I start reading. *The Birds of Dumfriesshire*, compiled in 1910 by Hugh S. Gladstone, suggests that the bean goose was more common but was being displaced by the pink-footed goose.[2] But all grey goose species look similar to some degree and even now, with modern knowledge and modern optics, identification is not easy. Early accounts are mired in confusion and misidentification. What is clear is that over the twentieth century the pink-footed goose became exceptionally common on the Solway Firth, where once it had been either irregular or unknown. The bean goose is now so rare in Dumfries and Galloway that if you see one you have to write a description of it for a panel of four men to adjudicate on whether you are correct.

I was dimly aware that pink-footed geese were supposed to be here in Dumfries, in the way that one is dimly aware of gravity or local politics: I know of the existence of these things and vaguely how they work and affect me, but that is it. Although, I can't imagine a time when I become obsessed with the machinations of councils or the essentials of physics, as necessary as they may be. I was not anticipating how frequently my thoughts would return to the geese, how my eye would be scanning the horizon for the smudge that betrays a skein on the horizon. I was not anticipating how much I would become obsessed with the geese. I was not aware how much they were becoming part of my life.

This is not unique to me.

People in Dumfries are friendly. The overriding first impression of the town is how much friendlier, more open to others, people are here. A neighbour sees me one morning heading out with my binoculars and telescope.

'You after th' geese?'

'Aye,' I say, wincing slightly. Scottish words jar with my English accent. I say the first half of the sound unthinkingly, then the second tends to die on my tongue.

That afternoon a man on a bus asks me where I've been. Birding, I say. His eyes light up. He's nae twitcher, he states, then details the way the whooper swans have arrived this past fortnight, and how they follow the geese upriver but don't get so far. He points at fields through the shuddering bus window: 'Geese in there this last week.' It's almost a shame to get off at my stop.

I work at a desk in my living room, facing the windows, looking out to the two lines of hills beyond the terrace roofs. It is a bleak, dreich day: October by calendar, deep into winter by spirit. I can only faintly see the first line of hills. The trees reduced to pale grey shadows, their shapes indistinct in the weather. I see a flock of geese again, swirling like static around the television aerials, descending down to the fields behind the houses.

I am bored. Unproductive. Sentences are forming in my head and dying at my fingertips. A blank Word document glares at me from my computer. I shut it. I'm out of the front door in a minute. Itching to see geese settled, to explore the subject of my new interest at closer range. It is hard to get an idea of a goose if all you ever knew of them was what you saw flying over or read from the bird books. It would be only half the picture. I want to anchor the skeins to the goose grazing in the fields.

Our flat lies at an odd angle. The view from our living room is to the southwest, not quite in line with the streets of the estate. The path zigzags between houses. It takes me to the road two fields north of where I want to be. I walk past the flock at first. They are hidden from the road by a fold in the land. It is only when a small skein, calling in flight, circles to join the flock that I notice them.

When geese detach themselves from skein and sky, they whiffle. Whiffling – its etymology lies in the movements of wind – is a ridiculous word for the way geese fling themselves upside down on the approach to land. It is how, as geese, they deal with the transition from flight; how a large, powerful bird, lacking the agility of other species, reduces height and speed. Their wings, hanging out, collecting air, act as a parachute. The geese drop down towards the field, vanishing into its green folds.

I cross the road and walk down a tiny farm track, beyond one cottage and towards a couple more. The track dips down to a boggy slack between patches of higher ground. I startle a snipe and it rockets out of the field with a single barked complaint. It flies off towards the geese, spread out on the low ground, near the burn that the map marks running through these fields. Another skein drops in, wings hanging out, geese descending. They land with their pink feet splayed out, on their short, stout shock-absorber legs. The pink is almost luminous in this weather. The flock is dense. A ribbon of geese: they are packed tight enough to obscure each other, and the flock seems to become as one, shuffling across the grass, a mass of gently moving backs, the occasional wary neck held up, a ball-of-socks head turning, looking out for danger.

I feel uneasy on the small track between cottages. I shuffle up to a tree and use it to obscure my movements from the wary geese. There's not enough verge to stand off the road and I hope the residents don't take me for a man acting suspiciously.

My scope is small and cheap and struggles with the light. The attachment to the tripod is wobbling, working itself loose. I scan the flock. Make an initial estimate of the numbers. I think it might be a thousand. All the geese I can see are pink-feet. This flock is large, but it is still a small percentage of those that come here. Half of the world's pink-footed geese spend their winter in Scotland.[3] Two-thirds of the world's population passes through on migration.

On land they are squat. They seem small, though they are not that small for a goose, just elegantly proportioned. They are slightly smaller than greylag geese and taiga bean geese. That realisation seems key: that geese are at once familiar and unfamiliar, known and unknown. Pink-feet are the species to start with, and not just because they are the commonest here. They are the base goose, the one from which the others deviate. Geese in Britain can be neatly divided into grey geese and black geese. Pink-feet are part of the *Anser* genus, the grey geese – though when I say 'neatly', I feel I should add that the grey geese are predominantly brown. Pink-feet are the rich, earthy brown of winter fields on their breast – a brown that gets darker to a peat-black head, the darkest part of their body and a useful distinctive difference from all except perhaps the bean geese. Their bills are short and triangular – slightly longer than they are tall, and dark as the earth they plunge them into, with just a window of the same pink colour as their legs. They have a brown back, but some have a frosty grey to it, which is not dissimilar to the dusty blush of pruinescence that grows on grapes and red cabbages. Underneath, behind the legs to the tail, is a patch of pure white that feels out of keeping with the rest of the brown. It feels like a mistake. It feels as if it should be a magnet for mud, but of all the geese I can see, it gleams unsullied on all of them.

I have a well-thumbed copy of Aldo Leopold's *A Sand County Almanac*: the spine was cracked years ago, and the corners of the pages are grubby and curling up at the tips, as if begging to be turned. There's an underlined sentence on most pages. It is one of the few books I return to repeatedly. This time for a newly familiar reason: a trio of geese honking from the cover and I am unable to resist delving in again.

I love the writing of Aldo Leopold. He is a man whose writing burns with a fervent desire for being outside and for being alive in a world with wildlife. *A Sand County Almanac* was written in the 1940s partly as a guide to the monthly changes happening in the environment around him – the sand county of Wisconsin, North America – and partly as a series of ecological essays that are astonishing in their insight and shocking for their continued relevance. It is a rare book – one I struggle to finish reading, but only because each chapter drives me outside, to engage with the world anew. Leopold had a land ethic. He felt that we should think like mountains. His thinking is radically ecological. He has a conception of the ecosystem and the trophic cascade that remains modern and relevant today and an easy way of expressing it that hasn't particularly dated. I notice the geese in his prose again. This is his evocation of March:

In the beginning was the unity of the Ice Sheet. Then followed the unity of the March thaw, and the northward hegira of the international geese. Every March since the Pleistocene, the geese have honked unity from China Sea to

Siberian Steppe, from Euphrates to Volga, from Nile to Murmansk, from Lincolnshire to Spitsbergen . . . By this international commerce of geese, the waste corn of Illinois is carried through the clouds to the Arctic tundras, there to combine with the waste sunlight of a nightless June to grow goslings for all the lands between. And in the annual barter of food for light, and winter warmth for summer solitude, the whole continent receives as net profit a wild poem dropped from the murky skies upon the muds of March.[4]

His geese are a different species, and going in a different direction from mine. I have always loved the way he sees them. They become a sort of United Nations – the world united, across borders, across political divides, through the diplomacy of geese, just existing. They are a reminder of the ecology that underpins everything, no matter what boundaries can be laid on top. He wrote this in Middle America, in the 1940s, his international geese defying the first flourishings of the Cold War, East versus West, us versus them. I find hope in the borderless world of birds.

I loved Leopold's March geese the first time I read it. I love it even more now that I am living on the flight lines of its equation. But perhaps equation is the wrong word: it is not a set constant. The deal does not come daily. Some days pass with no geese at all, some days end with a constant passing stream, skeins streaming past my living-room window as though it's a great goose highway. I think 'poem' is precisely the word for this. The way it takes unrelated tangible things – summer sun, some spare grain – and the way the results grow wings and transform into something incredible, unexpected and awe-inspiring.

But that isn't all of it. Leopold is asking us to consider geese in the vastness of time. They are a blip here at least. A metronome of the seasons, an artefact of the earth's turning. Condense time down and the geese here will disappear. It is a quirk, a trick of feeling that makes the rhythms of nature seem ancient and immovable. The pink-footed geese passing here are from the Icelandic population that has grown massively over the last century. Peter Scott and James Fisher – legends of birding – took an expedition into the heart of Iceland's central plateau in 1951, to locate the great unknown breeding location of pink-footed geese. They found them in late summer, when they were moulting their flight feathers, and the geese were unskeined, brought down to earth by their own temporary flightless state. They pioneered the technique that enabled them to catch and ring 1,000 pink-feet. Scott returned in 1953, and managed to ring 9,000 more. They speculate that this meant one-fifth of the world's population had been ringed. The latest survey of Icelandic pink-footed geese suggests that they've increased so much that the decimal point has moved: a population of 515,852.[5]

Leopold asks us to consider geese in a vastness of space. They make a mere hairline scratch on the area of our island nation. But they join us with the other North Atlantic islands and the lowlands of Continental Europe.

It becomes a sign that we are due to have visitors from the south. Torrential rain began the day before our friend Abby was due to arrive and carried on all the way through until the day she left. 'It doesn't look much like Scotland,' she says. 'I was expecting hills.' Sometimes you have to take the hills on faith: a trust that they are there and that the cloak of rain and swirling wind looks – and feels – a lot like Scotland anyway. The Nith is a river with an anarchic spirit. Where its banks were decided for it with bricks, it will overcome. It begins to flood, reclaiming the road and the park as its own territory.

We have learned that we cannot wait for good weather to do things. We have learned that to do and see anything here involves a good coat and a belligerence towards bad weather. Within reason. Abby is Cumbrian and she understands. We walk to the graveyard. As we cross the bridge over the river we see the inshore rescue boat shoot past, its blue light flashing, pilot and crew wearing flotation suits. Then police cars, the coastguard, the ambulance and the fire service, all thunder up the road, sirens and lights, heading to the weir. The word is that a kayak has been found overturned, no sign of a kayaker within. Briefly we don't know what to do. I am no good in emergencies. We carry on, chastened, not wanting to interfere, or worse, potentially cause another issue with a river that takes.

Suddenly – geese, pushed over by the weather, heading to the Solway. A chaos of pink-footed geese, stretching across the horizon. There are thousands, the skeins straggling, struggling without a set order, flying in all directions. Lead geese swapping with others. Individuals peeling off and joining other groups, geese like a kaleidoscope of panic. Their honking sounds urgent. Wings labouring, growing damp in the rain, energy sapped by the wind. I don't know where to look. It feels as if they have been swept up by the wind and scattered across the sky. I feel afraid for them. And helpless: the sirens of the emergency services blaring through gloom, the fragility of life – human and goose – exposed.

Miranda whispers in my ear that this is like the scene in *The Day After Tomorrow*, when the first sign of the apocalypse is a CGI sky filled with fake birds fleeing inland. But these are real birds. Cold and struggling, like us. Rain like this stings on impact with bare flesh, which the wind then chills to numb. My coat is good but the hood flaps about in windy conditions. My beard is sodden and my ears numb, my lips stiff with the cold. Abby is half frozen. We leave. The geese will make it away from town. It is not foggy so they will be able to find land to rest and roost on. But weather like this is draining. They cannot take too much bad weather.

We hear that the upturned kayak had been pulled loose and washed downriver by the flood. No one is missing. With the good news from the police our morbid feelings dissipate. Back into the warm embrace of our flat, we hang up coats, take off wet shoes, hang sodden socks over the radiators. Stick the kettle on: the reviving warmth of hot drinks all round. It feels good to go out in such weather, if only to feel the relief of coming home again. It convinces us that we can handle life up here with its legendary rain, and a climate tougher, more elemental than the gentle warmth of Essex. It is not a good idea to draw metaphors direct from the world of birds. But sometimes they are irresistible. Geese are becoming more than my totem – they are showing me how to survive the wind and rain and thrive in this area. Together we will be wintering.

2

Barnacle Geese

At the end of September we spent a day at the Wigtown book festival. Wigtown is a delightful town an hour's drive west of Dumfries, into the heart of old Galloway. It is delightful because it seems to consist entirely of second-hand bookshops, places designed to exploit my weaknesses for old maps and older bird books on labyrinthine shelves. They are expensive places – that stale scent of musty, mouldering old paper makes me want to spend the money that I should really be saving.

We returned to Dumfries in darkness, light smeared across the wet coach windows. Vibrant light. A funfair had sprung up alongside the river, fully formed and without warning, as if grown from rain on the soil of autumn pavement. It is called the Rood Fair and it has happened since the medieval period on the last Wednesday of September.

I didn't know then that it would coincide with the return of the barnacle geese.

A few weeks later I take the bus out of town. It feels time to explore our surroundings further.

The river is tidal as far as Dumfries. We get used to its slow breathing. The water inflating, deflating, flowing up, flowing out, another new rhythm adding life to a new place. South beyond Glencaple the river eventually opens out at Caerlaverock into a coastline of saltmarsh. The map is drawn with the landmarks here in the same shade of blue as the sea. What appears from land to be the sea is drawn on the map as brown mud, the channels of the Nith and Lochar Water and the Eden distinct, then braiding, interweaving, tracking into the channel of what the map finally defines as the Solway Firth, well west of where it stopped tracking the English–Scottish border. Perhaps this is an unfair description. How do you map a landscape that changes so utterly over the course of a day? How do you draw a boundary on something that changes size, shape and substance?

There are two Caerlaverock nature reserves, split in the middle by the ruin of a thirteenth-century castle. I head for the second one, run by the Wildfowl and Wetlands Trust (WWT). I get off the bus by the castle. A tiny farm road takes me to an old farm building, repurposed into a nature reserve visitor centre. *Caer* is a word of Celtic origins, meaning 'castle'. *Laverock* is old Scots for 'lark'. In spring I can see it would make sense: the landscape must be a constant symphony, a fortress of lark song. But not today. It is the aftermath of another autumn storm, beating itself out over the marshes.

The habitat of my heart is marshland. It feels good here. A mixture of the familiar and the new: familiar habitat and unfamiliar hills. Some familiar species and some unfamiliar words. I try one on my tongue: merse not marsh. It sounds good. The merse is grey-green, dulling to its vanishing point in the murk. The English border is lost in this grey, unusually beyond the range of visibility. In the hide I can feel the wind shaking the walls, funnelling through the open window, running through my thinning hair.

Halfway in the murk is a flock of barnacle geese. Today they are distant, nervous. Thousands arrived from their breeding grounds on Svalbard just over a week ago. They are feeding in weather they flew to avoid. The flock is dense and fringed with wary birds, their heads raised, cautiously observing. A sparrowhawk skims across the field, buffeted by the wind, tracked by the heads of geese.

Barnacle geese belong to the *Branta* genus. They are known as the black geese, which opens up a contradiction between the names and feathers of the geese. If the *Anser*, or grey geese, are more brown than grey, then the wild species of black geese in Britain are mostly grey.

For Barnacle geese the grey is a gradient from black to white. They are black at front and rear ends: their black wingtips concertinaed and tucked in over their black tail. Their neck is black, and so is their beak and eye, with a black line running between the two, through a white face. Thin black lines run down their back. Both sides of those lines are white and grey stripes. The grey stripes get broader the closer they get to the wingtips; the effect is a sliding from dark to light. Their flanks are a pale silver-grey that seems to reflect light. They shine in dull light and in bright light. It is the pale and not the black that stands out.

The Solway is filling with geese again, like the tides of the firth. It is gladdening. I look out for other birds as well, but they are mostly well hidden, lurking deep in the cover of bushes and ditches. It feels as if the wind is suppressing the true life of the place. I would have stayed on despite it, but I am subject to the whims of the bus timetable and I have to leave halfway through the day; and anyway we have a Tesco delivery due. I will be back. My marshy heart insists.

~

Most people have a story about how they became interested in birds. For Sir Peter Scott, it begins with his father, Robert Falcon Scott – Scott of the Antarctic. In March 1912, just days before he died trapped in an Antarctic storm with no supplies, he wrote to his wife, saying, 'Make the boy interested in natural history. It is better than games.'[1] It worked, eventually. When Peter Scott came to write his autobiography in 1961, he begins with the sentence, 'All animals have interested me, and birds more than others, but wild geese have an almost mystical importance.'[2] Scott found this mystical importance first through the barrel of a punt gun that fired half a pound of lead shot.

It was partly the challenge of it, the struggle between the innate wariness of geese and the hunter's need to sneak up on them, either by foot or floating in the punt. He described them as 'the most worthy quarry, to be placed far above any other fowl'.[3] But for Scott it was also everything else: the scenery, the otters, the owls and the other wildlife. The being at home in an unusual environment, thrilled by everything that winter by the marshes had to offer. I know what that's like.

The archives of *Country Life* magazine are revealing. Scott wrote articles about wildfowling that make a reader wince with the clarity of hindsight. In 1929 he recounted:

Memory recalls another great day. On a Scottish merse a pack of fifteen hundred barnacle geese was spending the winter ... My numbed fingers found the triggers and inexplicably pulled both at once ... I found that there were eight geese down: a great end to an exciting and exhausting stalk ... But there is always that one regret! Might I have brought down more had I fired the barrels separately? But, in all conscience, eight birds are enough.[4]

A year later he wrote, 'Barnacle geese, although the most beautiful in form and colour, are, without doubt, the stupidest of our geese.' This opinion, it seems, was based on their nervousness around people; something that feels understandable, given that Scott wanted to kill them. By the end of that article he restates his respect for the family, if not the species: 'But however stupid the greylag and the barnacle may be, the description is only relative: let it be remembered that a "wild goose chase" has not lost its meaning, whatever the species.'[5]

Within eighteen years of Scott's writing, the Solway Firth's barnacle geese were down to 300 individuals. All the barnacle geese that spend the winter here breed on Svalbard. The cause of their crash in numbers, according to the author W. Kenneth Richmond, writing in *Country Life*, without any apparent irony, was 'thanks almost entirely to indiscriminate shore-shooting'. On 1 January 1955 it became illegal to shoot barnacle geese. Richmond goes on to note in his article, written in 1961, 'I can vouch for the remarkable change that has taken place . . . on a recent visit I found that, on a conservative estimate, the number of Solway barnacles has trebled in the space of three years.'[6]

Scott had a hand in both the crash and the recovery. His legacy is one of a string of nature reserves around the country, and the WWT, a leading conservation organisation that he set up, as if as a penance for the wildfowling of his youth. Geese may have had a mystical importance for him; his importance for them is more tangible and earthy. It seems contradictory to hatch love out of the pursuit of slaughter. But then nothing about being human is necessarily straightforward. If anything, his journey reminds me of my teenage transformation from hapless fisherman to lover of nature. Hunting teaches the skills. The charisma of the species turns interest into love.

It did not take long for Scott to ditch the gun. By 1933 he was writing of his attempts to catch wild geese. When he founded the WWT after the Second World War, he would turn his interest in geese to the pioneering of captive breeding techniques for rare wildfowl, including the nene goose of Hawaii. By the time Scott had bred enough to reintroduce them, there were thirty in the world. By 2018, there were almost 3,000.[7] He records in his autobiography how the appeal of wildfowling was the relationship between man and bird: 'If it is the wildness of a bird which makes it attractive to outwit, it is in turn man's shooting habits which make the bird wild and difficult to outwit. So here is a complex between man and bird each part of which depends on the other.'[8] With the creation of the WWT, Scott maintained his relationship with geese; one founded around conservation rather than killing. A relationship less complex.

It was in 1970 that the WWT purchased the farm buildings, lands and merse to the east of Caerlaverock castle. In 1973 the Svalbard breeding grounds of the barnacle goose were protected. That their number was as low in 1948 as 300 now seems like a bad dream. By 2017 there were 42,600.

Although it is illegal to hunt some species of geese, there are still seasons for others, as well as culls and attempts at controlling populations. In an alarming piece of investigative journalism, the *Guardian* reported the number of licences that Natural England had granted between 2014 and 2019 to destroy individual wild birds and their nests and eggs. Most of these, the journalists glossed, were to prevent damage to crops, or to public health, vague as those terms are. Two in five licences granted were to enable the destruction of a greylag goose; over the five years, 67,586 individual greylags or their nests or eggs were destroyed.[9]

On the island of Islay, barnacle geese are now beginning to experience something similar. The population that spends the winter there breeds in Greenland. Like those on the Solway, they have increased as the species was protected and currently 42,000 spend the winter on the island.[10] It is, by all accounts, an impressive spectacle on a small island. Or perhaps it was. Scottish Natural Heritage (SNH) runs a licensing scheme that allows for the government's 'Islay Sustainable Goose Management Strategy' to include a target population of 25,000–30,000. This has led to the employment of marksmen shooting into the flocks of wintering geese, which might also contain the threatened Greenland white-fronted goose, a goose that it is illegal to shoot in Scotland.* The reasoning behind the cull is that the pressure of geese grazing on the grass has an impact on the farmer's ability to grow and cut silage. Despite this, and perhaps unexpectedly, analysis has found that there are 'difficulties in establishing any clear relationship between the amount of goose grazing and economic damage.'[11] SNH allows for a 'crippling rate' of 10 per cent. That is, geese shot but not cleanly killed. Those who escape the marksman's next shot, or can't have their necks wrung, are left to

---

* See Chapter 5, pages 138–9.

die slow deaths. In a statement to the investigative website, *The Ferret*, which published videos of the cull, SNH defended the cull as being 'best practice'.[12]

I come back to Aldo Leopold, who had a very different idea of what was meant by 'best practice'. *Round River* is a collection of Aldo Leopold's essays and journal entries. It concludes with his essay, 'Goose Music', where he returns to a favourite theme of his: the worth of conservation. He even calculates it: 'My notes tell me that I have seen a thousand geese this fall. Every one of these in the course of their epic journey from the arctic to the gulf has on one occasion or another probably served man to the equivalent of twenty dollars.'[13]

For Leopold, migrating geese offer irresistible symbolism: 'Another, passing over the head of a dark night, has serenaded a whole city with goose music and awakened who knows what questionings and memories and hopes.' They have gone from being nature's UN to something more personal – joy. And something that is worth looking after, because when it's gone, it's gone:

> Supposing there were no longer any painting, or poetry, or goose music? It is a black thought to dwell upon, but it must be answered. In dire necessity somebody might write another *Iliad*, or paint an Angelus, but fashion a goose? . . . Is it impious to weigh goose music and art in the same scales? I think not.[14]

His words take me back to October in the flat and the passing of pink-footed geese skeins. I think Leopold is right, even if $20 is a bit cheap. Geese are joy – worth conserving for that very reason alone.

I return to Caerlaverock in early November with Miranda and Dr David Borthwick. It is a polar-opposite day to the day of my previous visit. We are in the glorious beginning of winter, the crisp and calm after the autumn. There is deep-blue sky and wigeon whistling from the wetter areas, barnacle geese barking from the middle of the grass-green marsh, and a snipe shuffling through the brown rushes, visible then vanishing with the supreme confidence of camouflage.

David Borthwick is an enthusiast for the long nights and cold days of winter. Today is a little bit too bright and warm for him but the geese are good and this is his thing, his main area of expertise. He tells us more about the Rood Fair and the weird tangling of culture and geese in the history of Dumfries.

Dumfries has its likely etymology in the Gaelic *Dùn Phris*, meaning 'Fort of the Thicket'. Thicket is about right: finding information about the history of Dumfries is dense and thorny and impenetrable. The Romans came, conquered, then retreated behind their walls before eventually leaving Britain.

What they left behind in Dumfries is complex and contested, mired in the borders of the Anglo-Saxon kingdoms, Celtic tribes, Gaelic lands and Viking explorations. Dumfries is a border town: lowland and upland, freshwater and salt, Celtic and Anglo-Saxon.

A little way southeast of Dumfries is the small village of Ruthwell. Inside the pastel-painted walls of the church, the cultural thicket of all these borders is expressed in five metres of carved stone. The Ruthwell Cross is an Anglo-Saxon Christian monument, carved with religious imagery on every side and dating, it is thought, back to the eighth century. Around its edge is a Viking inscription, comprising in runes most of the text of a poem titled 'The Dream of the Rood'. It is included in some anthologies as one of the earliest examples of a Scottish poem, even if Scotland didn't exist back then.

Rood is an archaic word for 'crucifix'. The poem is a religious fever-dream: the crucifix on which Jesus was crucified comes alive and talks to the poet about theology. It is quite odd. Odder still: 'rood goose' is an old local name for the barnacle goose. The Rood Fair coincides with the Feast of the Exaltation of the Cross, which coincides with the arrival of the barnacle geese – the rood geese – to the coastal marshes of Dumfries.

The barnacle geese were probably here first. Hugh S. Gladstone writes of it as being the definitive goose of the Solway 'since the memory of man'.[15] They are older than religion or commerce, even if nobody thought to record their presence on the Solway and up the west coast of Scotland and Ireland until the twelfth century. Gerald of Wales, writing in *The History and Topography of Ireland* (1187), reports, 'I myself have seen many times and with my own eyes more than a thousand of these small bird-like creatures, hanging from a single log upon the sea-shore. They were in their shells and already formed. No eggs are laid.'[16] The curiosity is that what he was seeing was the goose barnacle, not the barnacle goose. There is a certain logic to this.

The problem of bird migration, unfathomable to the twelfth-century mind, had been partly solved by the assumption that these geese – noisy, obvious, charismatic presences of winter – must have hatched out of the barnacles that share their habitat. It explained their summer absence through the shape of the barnacle: a squat triangle, with two grooves running up it, like the bill of a goose. This meant that barnacle geese were not really birds at all, but fish, and conveniently could be eaten on Ash Wednesday and the Friday fast-days in Lent.* Until in 1215, at a Papal Council, when it became controversial enough for Pope Innocent III to rule that the barnacle goose was in fact a bird.[17] He knew what

---

* The Rood Fair is no longer held on Wednesdays, but now begins on a Friday. This may be more to do with commercial pressures than eating geese, however.

seems perfectly obvious now: that if it had feathers and flew it probably was not a fish. The myth of the barnacle goose's origins lingered longer than might be expected, in part because it wasn't until 1891 that it was apparently first found breeding in Greenland, by a man called E. Bay, a name that the twenty-first century has rendered untraceable. It wasn't until 1907 that barnacle geese were found breeding in Svalbard.[18]

With a mythology so fabulously strange and rich in human beliefs, it is easy to overlook the actual, living goose – born of eggs and definitely a bird, and defiantly normal. We are sitting in the furthest hide, the Merse Observatory. It is low tide. There are no geese, just four little egrets, and a view that stretches across the bay of the Nith from the Southerness lighthouse to the northern face of the Lake District fells. It is apparently Skiddaw, crowning the dark horizon, but this mountain and view are unfamiliar to me. The glistening layers of mud and water, striped and shining brightly, are hypnotic, and the space is sublime.

We head back via the other hides. A hare basks in the middle of a field, in front of a dense barnacle-goose flock, their monochrome plumage burning bright in the sun. The silver flanks dazzle, the white and black bars on their backs are like sharp light and thick shadow. The flock's movements are gentle, more relaxed than they were last month, more settled into their new half-year home. There are fewer heads held high on alert necks.

This day is glorious, spent in a way that feels completely right. We are like sponges, soaking up the peace of being in the outdoor stillness, the lives of birds unconcerned by our presence feeding and flying and being in the sun, as we are.

It was not to last.

November is the first month of the cold and the dark. It is the first depressed sigh of winter after the fireworks of autumn. Before the chill that we know should be coming with its consolations, we have to first get through the lukewarm and the wet. November's glorious beginning at Caerlaverock was a falsehood. We were lured into the expectation that it might be bearable, but then the rain comes and it feels as if we don't see the sun in weeks. And things slow down. We slow down.

We begin by learning to sleep again. Blackout curtains sealing the morning out, our bedroom becomes a space of almost permanent night. We sleep nine hours, then ten. Then doze in the darkness until we lose the morning. Alarms are easily snoozed. We do not feel rested. Opening the curtains on these days doesn't help. The sun is smothered by clouds, dimmed to the brightness of a low-watt lightbulb. We feel low-watt too. I never realised, in Essex, how solar-powered I am. I understand that if

I wake up and the rain is rattling the window panes, I might not want to go outside. But this is different. This is a sort of absence of weather, along with the absence of light. Cold but not cold enough. Tepid. In East Anglia my parents have woken up to frosts and we haven't yet. The days feel like an anaesthetic. November becomes numb. It is the first time I have ever struggled with winter.

It is Remembrance Day. We wake before our alarms, before dawn. Our friend Ollie, up for the weekend from London and, like all our visiting friends, the seeming cause of torrential rain the day before, begins to regret agreeing to this. None of us are used to the 6 a.m. start or our new panic-bought wellies.

We are up early for the dawn flight, a special event run by the WWT at Caerlaverock on certain winter weekends. It is a risk – it is always a risk with something as unpredictable as geese. The theory is, we are told, that we get to the merse before dawn, ready for the geese to awake and leave their roost. It might not happen. They might fly off towards a different part of the merse. It might start raining and they might not fly. It might never get light. The gamble is that we subject ourselves – and Ollie – to either cold, wet, insufferable boredom, or the spectacle of life waking up with the light.

We get a lift with David Borthwick through the dark. The car cuts a tunnel of light through the dark roads, headlights illuminating the eyes of deer, falling leaves and a river shining through the roadside field. As we approach the coast the light begins to creep in under the blanket of night. It is 6.30 a.m. The four of us stand by the weak light of the Caerlaverock visitor centre with a small group of visitors and three wardens. Some are holding torches, some are warming their hands on flasks of coffee. From the marshes around us redshanks shriek, curlews call, and early-rising whooper swans bugle through the darkness, freshly arriving with the winter from Iceland. The geese have yet to stir.

After a short talk – the obligatory disclaimer about the puddle-strewn state of the ground – we walk off along the avenues. I have never been beyond the last hide. It has always been out of bounds and it feels odd now, like trespassing, to go beyond the paths on a nature reserve, but the wardens are here as an assurance. We will not be disturbing the geese while they are guiding us, showing us the safe way.

The path beyond the last hide is concrete, a relic from the war, when the marshes were a firing range. My new wellies are loose and slap noisily on the ground, rubbing on my feet through two pairs of socks. The thin rubber conducts the cold. Through the slight light I can see Miranda and Ollie hunching into their coats, hands withdrawn into sleeves, necks sunk into shoulders: everything covered, everything cold.

We reach our end: a polygon of concrete slabs, veined with grass bulging through the gaps. We are hidden from the geese by a ring of gorse bushes, our silhouettes muffled, so we don't stand out as suspicious tall things against the flatness of the firth. It is 6.50 a.m. The river and the marsh are in absolute dark but the sky is relenting. Clouds are separating into thick strands like plumes of black smoke. The sky is deep navy, fading to the southeast and layers of ice blue and sandy yellow and amber just above the hills, a promise of the sun to come. Due south, glowing in the darkness, are the radio masts of Anthorn, thin thorn scratches in the night, dotted with bright lights, the red of freshly drawn blood. The Anthorn masts are transmitting signals to submarines – signals that are apparently unaffected by nuclear explosions. We are standing on old military ground looking at the new, and dreading, in the chill of the dark morning, its own small role in the machinery of apocalypse.

Light has been creeping in over the last hour. But when the sun finally breaks over the hill and through the strands of cloud, dawn becomes a rush. We look south and west, along the firth towards the lighthouse of Southerness, watching water and mud appear and grow light, streaked with dark lines of geese. Behind us whooper swans fly on to the marsh, calling always, trumpeting of the north. In Finland the composer, birdwatcher and nature-lover Jean Sibelius wrote in his diary, 'Lord God, what beauty!' after seeing sixteen whooper swans. He was not wrong. The birds are beautiful but there is a beauty to what we are doing as well. Standing, waiting: still while nature begins to move around us, the dark relinquishing.

Dawn is here. A thousand barnacle geese take off – flying towards and then veering away from us, flying over the last hide. There is no time to regret that the wardens didn't take us there instead. After half an hour of standing still in the first light, the birds come as if on the cue of dawn, as if flicked on by a switch of sunlight. Egrets fly past, fourteen little and one great white, dispersing into the gullies of the marsh to stand starkly white in muddy creeks. Through his telescope a warden picks out a peregrine falcon hundreds of metres away on the marsh, perched on a driftwood spire like a gargoyle, waiting for one duck's fatal false move. A ringtail hen harrier skims the ground along the seam of horizon. I shout about it but no one seems to hear. Everyone is busy watching, photographing, enjoying their own thing, their own long string of barnacle geese lifting off from the mud and flying to the merse each side of us, some overhead. The sound of their yapping calls – more beagle than bugle – is constant.

For David what we are seeing is a sign of constant metamorphosis. He has written of this place as a 'space of come and go ... ruled by the imperatives of flow'.[19] He thinks of the wintering birds – the barnacle geese and whooper swans – as examples of this ever present flow; the way their common names change from Scandinavian to British at some unfixed point on their migratory route; the way that the reserve here raises the flags of their origins to welcome in the migrants. David also reminds us of another eminence of Scottish literature. Sir Walter Scott, while writing *Redgauntlet*, says, 'He that dreams on the bed of the Solway, may wake in the next world.'[20] It is tempting, idly, before we have another coffee to get our brains going, in the drift of dawn, to wonder if it's true of the folklore of these geese too – bred on the Solway beds, hatched out of water into the world of land and sky.

Dawn changes constantly as well. At 7.23 a.m. – a band of intense yellow sun, strips of orange and pink cloud turning grey just out of the sun's reach. At 7.28 a.m. – the intense yellow dissipates to a puddle of buttery sun, surrounded by rosy clouds, pink strips of sky and the clouds that had been grey are now shot through with light and glowing indigo, with a promise of blue sky peeking out behind. At 7.37 a.m. – all intensity is gone, the sun shifts around behind the Lakeland fells, the clouds pink and dappled grey, more rolling in, snuffing out the blue, the yellow leaching out. The skeins of geese keep coming. The camera records them as wisps, a pale poly-winged smudge of geese in the now weakening light.

Gladstone thought that the barnacle geese were definitive of the Solway. He's right. Against the grasses of the merse, they stand out starkly. But against that green background they flock tightly, and anyway those on the edges are always anxiously looking out. They can't do that while sleeping. In the borderland of the light, somewhere between night and day, they make sense in the endless silver of the Solway. They are the colour of mud, water and rock. They are of the light.

I don't want to go. But we have to leave. It is all too rare that we get to slow down enough to watch the entirety of a sunrise, from dark to day. It feels special, particularly on Remembrance Sunday, a more meaningful, more poignant pause of reflection than that afforded by the planned pageantry in the town centre. We go for breakfast in the town's Wetherspoon pub. The old boys in tweed caps talking about Queen of the South FC have put on their dark regimental jackets, polished their medals. They suck their morning pints more sombrely than before.

A website tells me that seasonal affective disorder is a product of indoor lives, that despite the windows we are starved of daylight. It sounds like an appeal to nature fallacy to me, but at this moment I am willing to give it a go. A friend buys us a SAD lamp, a thin box that projects a bright white light. Our cat seems to like it and chooses to sit in front of it instead of on our laps. The instruction leaflet suggests we should sit and stare into it from a distance of 20 cm. We ignore that.

Turning it on as we wake up helps a bit. It performs a weird psychological trick on me. On my way back from the kitchen to make coffee, I see the light reflected out into the flat hallway and do a double-take. It has the brightness of actual sunshine creeping down a corridor. Only it's not, and I realise that when I re-enter the room, that there has been no miracle and the outside is still dulled. But I feel a little kick: a little shot of serotonin like a second espresso. I choose to write with it on in the corner of the room and I write for longer, the fog of this winter tiredness not gone, but delayed.

Maybe there's something in it. At least winters when I lived in London had their bright days, the office better lit than our house. My winters in Stirling were haloed in frost, ice-bleached to the bones, and the university library windows became a panorama of a frozen loch and sometimes snowy hills. The wind up the flat Forth valley was icy and energising for it. This November, it's a good day if I can see the line of trees on the hills beyond the houses. I settle for it looking like an old Chinese landscape painting: black trees and grey hills and a white background.

This numb November, I cling to the work I have to do, with an almost obsessive zeal. It's as if writing becomes my lifebelt, memories of summer islands keeping me from going under. I don't go outside much at all. My goose-watching retreats indoors, and skeins of pink-feet are less frequent than they were in October. One day I am doing the washing-up while mostly looking out of the window as the light cracks through, sweeping away the gloom, a mackerel patterning to the sky. Clouds over the hills on the horizon look to be lenticular. I watch twelve collared doves line up on our telephone wire, bobbing tails to keep balance, like notes on a stave on the paper of a pebble-dash terrace. The hills turn hazy. It is late afternoon. I walk out and back through the park at dusk, a blackbird calling loudly in each bush either side of the path. It is the most evocative sound of winter, their *pink-pink* scolding like an act of resistance against the coming darkness.

An email brings news that there is an elusive goose. One that should be out on the Solway, but has never been seen here. The WWT doesn't know where it spends its winters. But it is a goose that I have seen before, elsewhere.

It was March 2015. Every few days I had been distantly seeing a flock of six barnacle geese that had spent some of the winter in the fields of North Ronaldsay, Orkney. They were always a field or two away, lurking behind cows or distantly on the lochs. I was told that the winter had been long, that winters always are on the northern isles. Cold, but not really freezing. Regular rainfall. The grey-green grassy fields are churned up and muddy, black and slippery as ice. By mid-March the weather had improved. We even had a sunny day, full of lark song and the first migrant birds. I was delighted. I briefly walked out in a T-shirt to soak up the light and slight heat, cycled up to the northern headland of the island. Walking along the bouldered coastline, I poked my head to look over a short sward of grass in front of a loch. And saw the six barnacle geese closer than I had ever seen a wild goose before. I caught my breath. Crouched awkwardly. Tried to melt into my background, aware that geese are wary beings and that any sudden interruption to the landscape could make them fly and disappear for days.

In retrospect, I don't know why they didn't fly. The day felt special to me. It was the first glimpse of the difference that the sun made to the island, the first feeling that this was a sort of paradise. And ludicrous though this is, I can't rid my mind of wondering if it was special for them too. As if the sun running suddenly strong through feathers was pleasurable enough to coax them into a sort of confidence, a reluctance to fly. Closer than ever before, I watched them through binoculars, noticing a light-green ring on the right leg of one, with the letters ZSP.

I reported it to the WWT. They put me in touch with the Dutch ringer, who had attached the ring to its right leg in August 2012 when it was a young gosling, near the world's northernmost civilian settlement on the island of Spitsbergen, Svalbard. He told me that she was a female, that she had subsequently gone missing, and not been seen again on North Ronaldsay or at any of their more usual spots. I later find out that she was seen in Andøy, Norway, in May 2015, then a week earlier the next year in the same place.

Geese tend to stick with their habits but sometimes they do break their traditions. In the

Netherlands, barnacle geese are increasingly staying and breeding in the places where they spend the winter, instead of returning to breed on the Russian island of Novaya Zemlya, at the far northeast corner of Europe. Scientists suspect that this is to do with the adults delaying their return migration. Geese usually migrate as families for the first round trip, but the adults' bond with the young has a time limit and if they delay, the goose family unit can dissolve before they have returned to Russia. This, it is thought, has led to the young staying to fend for themselves in the Netherlands. But there is a bonus to this: the scientists also note that those that shun the two-thousand-mile flight and stay, were much more likely to survive.[*21] There are barnacle geese flocks growing on the Suffolk coast that contain birds likely to have escaped from captivity. Among

* Those that stay had an annual survival rate of 97 per cent. For those that migrated, that fell to 55 per cent.

them, ringed wild barnacle geese have been found in the middle of the breeding season, very far away from Svalbard, where they would be expected to be at this time of year.[22]

I wonder if geese dream, during the dreary dreich of Scottish Novembers, of the jagged peaks of Norway, and the perpetual daylight of the Arctic summer, growing the green-brown grass of the tundra. I wonder why this goose, in North Ronaldsay, has never been seen on the Solway. Whether she is just elusive: a lurker on a little-visited marsh, or hiding her legs in plain sight. Or whether she is a trailblazer or a traveller or just in search of different places.

～

November bleeds greyness into December. December's dampness begins to freeze. Fog spends several days cloaking the street, shrouding the graveyard over the road. I walk through it – an impromptu Gothic wonderland – and down to the footbridge over the river, visibility so low that I can't see either bend and it feels as if I am trapped in a cloche, my own bubble of the world, everything else dulled, hidden or gone. At night along the road it is possible to see only the streetlamps, and the way the freezing fog curves out from and defines their light, until it looks like a low-vaulted ceiling, the world a cloister of light strung up by each lamp post.

Two weekends before Christmas I finish my first book. I submit it to my publisher, nervously writing out an email that might change my life some months later, might not. I play loud music through my headphones to coax the words out, for the injection of faux bravery it gives me. I press 'send'.

And as soon I do, the *wink wink* sound creeps through, under the headphones, intruding on the music. I push my headphones off, run to the window. There is a huge skein, spread out, uncountable but easily into the multiple hundreds. Chevron upon chevron. A large triangular skein, braiding out, and back-filling, running like a river into a delta. Skeins within a skein of pink-feet flying directly over our flat, unusually low, unusually direct, unlike anything I had seen when they were passing daily in autumn.

The Romans and Greeks of ancient times used to use the movements of birds to predict the future. And I understand, sometimes, what they were thinking, when they looked on the flight of birds and saw an augury.

3

Greylag Geese

I feel as though I have migrated in my mind. In finishing the book, carrying out the agonising last read-throughs, my head has spun around the British Isles and its islands, following seabirds in the thick of spring and summer. Pressing 'send' dumps me back in the middle of winter without much left to do. I dread finishing. I have a habit of work, a project on the go, always, an intellectual fixation with which to exhaust myself. Without a project, I am just lethargic, exhausted without reward.

Miranda and I head back to southern England to share Christmas with our families: first mine, then Miranda's. It is our week of being like geese, who spend the winter in their family groups. Independent from a young age, geese (and swans) typically remain as families for the entire yearly cycle that is avian life: from hatching to the beginning of the next breeding season. Some families stick together even longer. It has been found that this leads to improved survival for geese, in turn leading to a more productive breeding season the following summer. But in each goose flock there is also a social structure. The larger the family unit, the more dominant those geese will be: adults without young are the weakest in the flock. David Cabot, the great Irish wildfowl biologist, compares geese to elephants because of this, the way the young are brought up, trained by the flock. And I like the idea: geese as the megafauna of the winter marshes.

We, on the other hand, moved very far away from our families, because Scotland has its hooks in us. When I've been in a Scottish phase of life before, Christmas has been one of the few times that we can behave like geese, with the family coalescing again, coming together to eat and drink and look out for each other.

Suffolk and Bedfordshire. We take the extra daylight of being south and east with glee. Half an hour of morning light, and although the sun sets at the same time in the afternoon, it sets differently. The long Scottish twilight behind the hills to the west has gone, replaced by the twilight-permeable tangle of oak trees. The light lingers here, even on the solstice. From my parents' house, I head out to Lackford Lakes, a local reserve where I first learned the differences between birds. I watch the gulls streaming in to roost, swirling like a spindrift over the pale water turning dark with the bodies of resting birds. I watch them until it is twenty-five minutes after dark and the visitor centre has shut and I have no idea where the afternoon went.

It is a warm Christmas in Bedfordshire. Christmas Eve dawns with fog clinging to the branches, the dew beneath bejewelling the lawn. The fog lifts by midday and we walk across the green to the farm over the road, where half the hamlet and its surrounding villages seem to have turned up at the same time to collect their Christmas meat. The track is rutted and pot-holed, puddles reflect the sky and people in high-vis jackets direct cars to places to park. We join a talkative queue. I am about to experience a sort of cognitive dissonance. We are here to collect a goose, an act that I think will change my relationship with geese.

I do worry about the implications of eating an animal that I profess to love. We treat wild animals and domesticated animals very differently. I am told that the farmer's family once kept a goose back as a pet and named it. One year, it was accidentally sent for slaughter with the rest of the flock, the cause of much sadness on the farm. I could not, in my current circumstances, bring myself to pick up a gun and shoot at a wild goose, or any goose, or bird, or animal. Isn't it hypocritical of me to wash my hands of it, and let the farmer take his geese to slaughter so I don't have to see it? The moral quandary is Christmas indigestion for the mind.

Eating goose at Christmas has been a family tradition on Miranda's side that has survived forty years, house moves, vegetarian children and the free-range flock spending the summer on the fields at the back of the house, their honking part of the soundtrack to summer in the garden. The walk to collect the goose always used to be Miranda's tradition, just her and her father, and now I am an intruder. She insists she's happy with me joining them, even as I become a startling reminder of change and the passing of time. In the farm we are served by the children that Miranda used to babysit, and the woman who used to tease her for being a vegetarian.

Bringing the goose back in its white cardboard coffin, we are stopped briefly by a chicken, a mad-eyed clucking dinosaur of a bird, strutting through the grass by the gate it had somehow scuttled through. I look up, through the lace of bare willow branches at a high fluff of white clouds, like smeared dust on a sky of pure, blue clarity and the day looks perfect. The sort that justifies any winter bleakness.

Half past two. Christmas afternoon. The cats are lurking in torn wrapping paper, having spent the past week fighting over presents that aren't for them. The goose is carved, after cooking for most of the morning. Its meat is dark and rich – and, yes, delicious. Maybe it's the soporific atmosphere of Christmas encouraging me not to think, but I don't feel like a hypocrite for eating it. It feels like another way of appreciating a species, and while I wish it hadn't had to die, it feels right to make a celebration of it, to be respectful of its life. I wouldn't want it regularly: I have a low meat diet and I want it to stay that way, for my own health as well as the good of the environment, even if this domestic goose had a life in the fields as close to the wild as it could get without migrating.

The taste of goose, in the form of the domesticated bird, is about three thousand years old in China and Egypt. Eating one can be a reminder of old ways of living. In Michael Shrubb's masterful yet horrifying book, *Feasting, Fowling and Feathers: A History of the Exploitation of Wild Birds*, he finds enough evidence to say, 'Wildfowl – the swans, geese and ducks – were, and possibly still are, the most important group of wild birds to humanity, providing food, feathers and, latterly, sport.'[1]

There are geese in the archaeological remains of Roman Britain. Domesticated birds – poultry and geese – consumed or sacrificed, then dumped in the midden.[2] This is true also of Saxon Britain. However, although we can see evidence of the presence of geese back then, it is not until the medieval period that the remains of geese in archaeology become common, revealing the importance of goose to the diet of the period.[3] In the fifteenth century, at a feast to inaugurate the new archbishop of York, 2,000 geese were eaten, along with 400 swans.[4] A century earlier King Richard II had a feast with 200 geese and a mere 50 swans. Swans were often skinned, roasted, then the skin replaced around the roasted meat, as a grotesque centrepiece. Geese were not special enough to merit such treatment. That they significantly outnumber swans when they are both on the menu is testament to this.

To supply the birds in large enough numbers for such gargantuan feats of consumption, geese had to be domesticated and farmed. Hunting for wild geese as we or Peter Scott would understand it did not begin in earnest until guns were accurate enough to hit a small flying target. Before this, wild geese would have been caught in summer, in the period when they are briefly flightless while they moult their wing feathers.

The species that was domesticated – and eaten – in the West was the greylag goose. Greylag is the alpha goose, the type species. Its scientific name, *Anser anser*, translates as 'goose goose'. There are three distinctive populations in Britain: those that breed in Iceland and spend the winter here; those that breed on Scotland's lochs; and those that never leave the comfort of ponds and lakes, with a ready supply of bad white bread for them to feed on, as familiar to us as introduced species such as the Canada goose.

For something so important to human history – for a bird so big, loud and obvious – greylag geese are a surprisingly dull species. Jeremy Mynott, eccentrically, curates a list of the birds that have this absence of charisma: he includes the greylag alongside the Canada goose, coot, woodpigeon, pheasant and greenfinch as species that 'do not have that combination of qualities that give the fizz'.[5] I don't agree with the whole list, but the greylag has become a suburban, semi-tame bird, devoid of the wild charm of other species. It does not help that it is a thickset bird, a goose that lacks elegance, with its big body cloaked with a muddy grey-brown plumage, the colour of concrete. Its bill, again big, is an orange that slides into pink at times. Those that grow up on park lakes often survive on a diet of bread. Bingeing on bad bread when young can affect the growth of the bird's wings – twisting out from its body instead of lying flush against it. This leaves the geese flightless, something that usually cuts their life short. It is known, innocently, as angel wing.

Goose meat remained a popular part of the human diet for centuries; it was the bird traditionally eaten at Christmas until it gradually started to be replaced by the turkey. Even in the eighteenth century, two centuries after the turkey was introduced to Britain, the farming of geese was still common. The writer Daniel Defoe, in his *A Tour Through the Whole Island of Great Britain*, talks about the droving of poultry, particularly of geese from Norfolk to London – a wing-clipped walk for the geese.[6] I find it hard to imagine how this was achieved, how hard it must be to herd a flock of belligerent, self-willed animals such as geese. A fascinating glimpse into goose droving is provided by an eighteenth-century bet between Lord Orford and the Duke of Queensbury, as to whether it was quicker to herd a flock of geese or a flock of turkeys. Orford won: the geese, it is said, completed the journey from Norwich to London two days sooner as they did not stop to sleep, whereas at dusk the turkeys went to roost in roadside trees.[7]

Domesticated geese vary in colour, and this affects their meat too. The grey birds grow more slowly but apparently taste better; the white birds eat more quickly and convert grain to meat faster and therefore taste inferior.[8] Goose is an awkward meat. It is both fatty, so makes a mess when cooked (though what is Christmas without a mountain of clearing up and cleaning), and big boned, producing surprisingly little meat for the price compared with other poultry. This means its popularity has declined in favour of cheaper, more plentiful food sources. *Country Life* magazine reported in 2018 that the British eat only 200,000 geese at Christmas, compared with 10 million turkeys.

Raising a goose for meat produces a useful by-product: feathers. Historic quotations out of context can sound splendidly eccentric: Shrubb records that during a fifteenth-century war 'six feathers from every goose in 20 southern counties were ordered to be sent to the Tower by March 14th', which sounds

like a tax that is both surreal and unusually specific.[9] But the feathers were needed for the fletches
of arrows, important ammunition at the time. It was
goose feathers helping the arrows of the longbow
archers fly at the battle of Agincourt.

Goose feathers were also used as quills, the
cheap, disposable pens of the period. The user would
cut and recut nibs into the feather shaft as they
were worn away with the act of writing. The word
'pen' comes from the Latin for feather, *penna*. The
American Declaration of Independence is supposed
to have been signed with a quill taken from a goose
breed appropriately known as the 'pilgrim'.[10] William
Shakespeare would have used quill pens to write his
plays, and there's a nice circularity that he would
have used one for writing his Agincourt scene in
Henry V. Goose feathers complicit first in violence
and then in art.

Another use for feathers has proved more controversial. Down feathers lie close to a bird's body

under the main layer of feathers. They make good insulation for humans as well as birds, particularly in jackets that are popular with climbers and hikers. The majority of the feathers used in down jackets come from goose farms in Hungary and China, where the birds are raised for meat and foie gras, a pâté made from the fatty livers of geese that have been force-fed maize (usually with a tube, which most would consider an act of unconscionable cruelty). Geese are also plucked alive for their down feathers, which is stressful and painful as a feather that is not ready to moult is attached to follicles in the skin. The animal welfare charity Four Paws states that this can be done up to sixteen times in the lifetime of a farmed goose.[11] There are signs of improvement: manufacturers of down jackets, having been exposed and shamed by animal-welfare charities, are now putting into place schemes to protect the geese, refusing to use down from birds that are live-plucked or involved in the production of foie gras.

There was another use for a goose, illustrated by a famous scene from Roman history: the legend of Juno's sacred geese, birds that supposedly lived in her temple on the Capitoline Hill of Rome. In 390 BCE, with Rome invaded by the Gauls, the holy hill was surrounded. The Roman historian Livy records that neither the human guards nor the guard dogs noticed the Gauls slipping into the final, unconquered part of the city. Only the temple geese stirred. Livy writes, 'The geese were their salvation, for with their loud honking and the clatter of their wings they woke up Marcus Manlius.'[12] The attack on the Capitoline Hill has been carved into reliefs and painted many times, and the geese stand, wings stretched out, a footnote to history.

The guard geese of Rome find an unusual counterpoint in the 'Scotch Watch': a flock of Chinese geese given the job of guarding the Ballantine's whisky warehouse from 1959 to 2012.* Online there is silent film footage of the flock of predominantly white and two grey geese. The footage is undated but I suspect it was shot around the time of their introduction. They are alert: rearing up, necks outstretched, heads raised high. In another clip they run after a man dressed in black, wings flapping, futile without their flight feathers, which have been clipped to keep them there. It is odd seeing them silent, knowing the racket they must be making. Sadly, technology catches up with even the best of geese, and they were apparently retired to Glasgow Green. I've walked around the green, a large swathe of grass near the city centre. By the river, I saw two Chinese geese – one white, one grey. They saw me and instantly stood up and started honking exceptionally loudly. I can't know if they were members

* A video of the geese in action can be seen here: https://www.youtube.com/watch?v=vubAxSpoIao

or descendants of the 'Scotch Watch', but it certainly sounded as if they could have been.

⌄

I become grumpy around Christmas time. Over-fed and hungover, the anxieties of presents and pleasing people fizzles out into further lethargy, a short-circuiting of patience. I struggle with myself and why I am not the vegetarian or vegan that I think I probably should be. Days stretch out. The gap from Boxing Day to Hogmanay feels like a whole year in itself. The second dog days, the year waiting to be put out of its misery.

Every Christmas a pile of bird books appears beside me. It renews itself annually. I bury myself in it. This year it's *The Snow Goose*, a short fable by the American author Paul Gallico. Written in England, in 1941, it concerns war and redemption, around a figure who is a thinly veiled portrait of Peter Scott.

A friend advised Scott he could probably take legal action but he decided not to pursue it, instead agreeing to illustrate the British edition. Seventy years later the WWT published an anniversary edition with Scott's original illustrations. As a fable it is moving. As an animal story, it ends in tragedy, as they all seem to, but its depiction of birds is strikingly authentic. It gets to the heart of a modern human relationship with geese: the way they symbolise the transformation of the seasons, and the associations of growth and death and change, for us as well as for the landscape. Like the lead character, Rhayadar, the snow goose is lost and out of place, both of them outcasts. After Rhayadar's death the last sighting of the goose is as it flies off high, 'no longer the snow goose but the soul of Rhayadar'.

I don't know if the poet Mary Oliver knew of *The Snow Goose* – it seems a better bet that she knew of Leopold's geese from *A Sand County Almanac* – but one of her best-known poems,

'Wild Geese', takes a similar subject, the environmental rhythms revealed by the passing of migrating flocks of geese, and the consolations they provide for a fractious mind. For Oliver it's the insistent sound of the geese – Leopold's 'wild poem' – that reminds her of her own place in the world. The passing of wild-geese flocks has a familial quality for her, a reminder of the relatedness of all things. Leopold's geese connect one nation to another, Oliver's bind people to place, and Gallico's create an emotional identity between man and creature. Writers seem to perceive in skeins a powerful metaphor for unity.

~⌣~

Our long-standing appreciation of geese means that they crop up regularly in art and myth across civilisations, stretching far back in history. One of the oldest seems to be *The Geese of Meidum*, a painting

from Ancient Egypt, from around 2500 BCE,* showing a pair of white-fronted geese lined up with a
pair of bean geese and a pair of red-breasted geese,
as if they were taking part in an identity parade or
posing for an early Egyptian field guide. There is
absolutely no doubt about their identification: on
the white-fronted geese the barring on the breast
is visible, along with the white blaze behind the bill,
the orange legs and the dark back. They have smaller
bodies than the bean geese. It is a remarkable piece
of observation. I find the clarity of it exceptional
and moving. It's tempting sometimes to think birding, or an appreciation of wild birds, is a relatively
recent thing: this is evidence that refutes that utterly.
My love of geese might be recent, but it connects

---

* An aside: this is, I think, remarkably similar to the hunting
lodges in Scotland that cover their walls in images of their
prey – a combined and difficult love for the animal and the
act of killing it.

me with a human fascination extending back for millennia.

In Homer's *The Odyssey*, when Penelope's suitors take advantage of Odysseus' absence, she dreams of them as the twenty geese that she keeps at her house, which are then suddenly, violently, killed by an eagle. Odysseus takes the hint and kills the suitors. While this is perhaps not great PR for geese, it is evidence of their importance to human life that they have a role in one of literature's earliest and greatest stories.

Edward Armstrong speculates in *The Folklore of Birds*, that 'the goose may have been revered before it was domesticated' due to its frequent appearance in early religious art and symbolism.[13] Take, for example, the first Scottish depiction of a goose. It comes from an eighth-century Pictish grave, from the farmlands of Moray, now preserved and on display in the labyrinthine National Museum of Scotland: the Easterton of Roseisle stone.

Originally it was the top slab of a stone coffin, and its underside is carved with two animal symbols. Below, a grinning salmon, carved with clarity, stretching almost across the width of the stone. Above, a goose looking back over its shoulder, its eye comically big, its body rotund, convincingly goose-like. Behind the legs, a line to indicate the patch of white, and four lines above it, the primary feathers folded up, and held above the tail.

There is no way of knowing what goose it is. Considering the location, on the Moray Firth, it could be greylag, barnacle, brent or pink-footed. My gut instinct says it is a small goose. I want it to be barnacle; I feel the shape is more correct, though this is completely unprovable. And there's nothing to suggest that the Picts recognised the individual species of goose.

Why a goose? And why a salmon, for that matter? I have no idea. We do know that salmon and geese are two of the most charismatic migratory animals of the Scottish countryside. Both offer a seasonal bounty of rich meat – if you can catch them. Both animals are powerful, elusive and shy. This comes across in the carvings: the salmon is boldly defined, almost shark-like in the way it exudes power. The goose is looking back over its shoulder, naturally watchful, like the guard geese of Rome.

It feels important to me that they are both migratory animals and it seems fitting that this should come from a grave. It makes me think of the psychopomp of Greek mythology (*psyche* for 'soul'; *pompos* for 'conductor'), the animal that guides souls from their moment of death to their place in the afterlife – as the goose seems to do at the end of Paul Gallico's *The Snow Goose*. It was a role that animals were thought to be particularly good at. Perhaps the carving represents something of this kind. We know little about the Picts, but I find this speculation irresistible.

Finally we return to Scotland for Hogmanay but I spend it alone. I walk around the local park on the last evening of 2018, watching the gulls drift south towards their estuary roost and vanish in the gathering gloom, while the sky turns icy, purple, cool and crisp.

I want the year to end with a skein of geese and my last birds seen or heard: as fitting an end as any that I can think of to something as arbitrary as a year. But it doesn't work like that. Nature does not usually supply a conveniently neat coda. Instead I watch a steady stream of black-headed gulls twist through the lengthy twilight, until it becomes too dark to see.

4

Brent Geese

I wake, mysteriously free from the hangover that I'm dimly certain I deserve. Dawn is glowing at the curtain's edges, the sunlight irresistibly asking to be let in. It is 1 January and everything is hushed and stilled at a time of the morning when people are usually active. The shutter is down on the shop opposite our house. Nobody walks. All the curtains are still pulled shut. The clarity of this early morning is crystalline, the sun as if washed, spick and span and ready for the new year and there's only one thing I can think to do. Alone, I head to the river.

The path along the river tracks southeast and I am almost blinded by the intensity of the sun. Usually this makes me grumpy. I don't wish for it to be turned down today. The blue of the sky and the green of the fields is vivid and intense and it feels good to be alive in the exquisite clarity of it all. The landscape is charged with the energy of the light.

The next day is also a bank holiday in Scotland and the sun remains, the sky stays clear and the temperature plummets. A hoar frost forms, thick and sparkling, a dew that transforms into a cold white fur on everything that spent the night outside. The dead stems of umbellifers, grasses and spiders' webs are given new life by the thick white frost, their lines emphasised by the clinging cold.

We walk up the slope; through the side bushes along the path we get a panorama of frozen fields below, the grass bleached and scorched by the cold, an iced stream, a flock of sheep huddling together and the shadows filling in the gentle folds and dips between the fields. The consolations of the cold. This is what I have been waiting for all winter. The crispness that comes with frost and ice. The exceptional, vivid clarity of the day. It makes Dumfries feel like a place apart from the numbness of November and December's dire murk. It would be bad science to conclude from a sample size of two but I'm going to risk it: January already feels better.

I'd been thrilled to return to Scotland and my new winter companions, but a fortnight later the pink-feet seem to have stopped flying over the flat, finding other ways over or around the town to get to the fields they feed in. Starved of their company after only just having started to appreciate them, I have become greedy for birds: more geese, more flocks, more species. It is almost as though I feel the need to make amends for my past apathy. If they won't come to me, I will go to them.

In the morning I begin to plan a road trip in my head, working out where else geese spend the winter in Britain, while navigating a moraine of paperwork. I juggle job applications and goose guides, reports of sightings and unfolded maps. I could travel to Stranraer and stand on the shore of Loch Ryan, where a small flock of pale-bellied brent geese spend the winter. But that is two and a half hours by bus, and the prospect of tying myself to a public-transport schedule when trying to seek out something as independent and as bloody-minded as a goose doesn't appeal. Although I love Scotland, my East Anglian roots nag at me, the marshes pulling me back across the country. And if it's brent geese I want to see, there's nowhere better than my child-hood home to find them, even if they are the more common dark-bellied variety.

The afternoon offers me a two-hour window before another Tesco delivery and I gratefully take the opportunity to escape outdoors. There still don't seem to be any geese around as I retrace my footsteps from New Year's Day, but I console myself with the whooper swans as I walk along the river, enjoying the rare winter light.

The sun is falling and its light is catching in the dead grass by the riverbank. The brown becomes golden and the far bank becomes stripes of golden grass and dark shadow and black trees. The river becomes a pale mirror. A blemish in the river catches the corner of my eye. A dark shape in the light water that quickly disappeared. I blink, and the dark shape resurfaces again. It looks around. Takes a second. Then slips underwater, leaving a vanishing tail, no splash and no wake. Otter!

My heart rate races. I have seen otters before but here – here is a surprise. It is swimming towards the town, slipping between the human world and the underwater world, seamlessly, silently moving, slightly faster than walking pace and only a few metres away from the riverbank. I walk with it a short while, as it continues its routine of head and tail, slipping in and out of the golden water, still seamless, except for one little, dolphin-like leap.

Time gets the better of me. Reluctantly I walk away from the otter, and dash home to meet the Tesco delivery. I get to my front door as the delivery driver does. 'That was lucky,' he says, and I think he doesn't know the half of it.

Seeing an otter is thrilling – particularly because normally they are so hard to spot. Unlike geese, usually. If you set out to see geese, you will almost always see them in the right place. They are stubborn and equally wild but they find it harder to hide. It is perhaps a reason why when I was younger I found them easier to ignore. But now that I'm ready to take notice, they seem to have disappeared. Despite their absence, they are at the front of my mind, inescapable. Geese in the cortexes. Skeins in the synapses.

A day of trains. Into London and out again and back to my parents' house in Suffolk by darkness. I want to return to my old places, to make amends for my old lack of interest. I want to repopulate my memories, vividly, with the geese that were always there in the background of winter.

Geese like space, marshes and mud and there's plenty of that up the coast, rivers and hinterlands of Suffolk, Essex and Norfolk where 98,000 dark-bellied brent geese can be found.[1] There are two types of brent geese that spend the winter in Britain, breeding in three different locations. Pale-bellied brents either breed on Svalbard and winter in Northumberland, or breed in Canada and winter in Northern Ireland (and in small numbers on the west coast of Scotland). Dark-bellied brent geese, meanwhile, breed in Arctic Russia and winter throughout the muddy parts of south and east England. From the breast up they are essentially identical.

My dad is coming goosing too – he is, after all, to blame for my love of birds. He drives and I do not. He also has a subscription with BirdGuides, a company that texts you information about goose and other bird sightings in your area, and I do not. We have a plan but we are at the mercy of the weather. Tonight the temperature is plummeting and the wind is swinging northeast and we can't be sure what this means, other than that it will be cold. Cold weather has a tendency to move birds around, to shuffle the pack of waterfowl. Ice seals their food and habitat away from them. If it's worse in the rest of Europe, particularly in the Netherlands, it will bring a large amount of wildfowl over the North Sea to escape the cold. If it's worse here, it will move our birds on to the warmer southwest. This could be absolute success or abysmal failure.

It is 7 a.m. Feathers of ice fan across the car's windscreen. The full moon is high in the pale-blue dawning January sky. Dad is driving through a luminous morning, and I am watching the passenger window framing the sun, rising up to meet the lingering moon. A thin mist is folded along the creases of the fields, above the green baize of winter wheat. Along the fields, a line of oaks like ink, blotched with mistletoe. Clouds are striping the sky blue and white as we enter northeast Essex.

It is the last we shall see of the sun this morning. As we drive through Tendring the sky clouds over. The car thermometer records the temperature dropping. We head towards Walton-on-the-Naze, taking the back roads to the edge of town.

We park up by the Naze Tower, an old navigational aid for ships on an outcrop of high ground. It would do no good now. A haze has descended, somehow, despite the car trembling with the buffeting wind that tries to snatch the door from my hand. I scurry around to retrieve my coat from the boot, hiding in scarves, hats, coats, gloves, five layers of clothing for the temperature that, with wind chill, feels every bit like the forecast −5°C. It is winter in the raw, weather geese are better built to deal with than we are.

The grass is frosted but the mud is still slippery under foot as we walk down the slope through the lingering haze, towards the tip of the Naze and the marshes that lie beyond. At the bottom of the slope, the path leads us down an old sea wall, salt-marsh to the north, green fields and cattle grazing and reed-lined ditches of frozen water to the south. It is a quintessentially Essex part of the coast here. There is a sense of disorder and energy; death and life. Land eroded with each tide yet still populated with grey plover, redshank, dunlin. A sanderling sprints down a thin strip of sand beyond a token, broken concrete sea wall. The headland here, now behind us, is comprised of the dead things of pre-history: the fossils of the Eocene, the Pliocene and the Pleistocene.[2] But this land is also made of out of life, which can be recovered at low tide, where the cliff crumbles into the sea. Each chunk taken out of the Naze forms new land further down the coast. Each tide reveals new fossils, new mud and new food. This is new life for the birds of these marshes.

Our first sighting is false. A skein of imposters. A long string of cormorants, black against the grey sea, flying away from us, at an angle that obscures their identity, until a second closer string of cormorants catches up and I realise my mistake. Low tide means expansive mud, extra land for the geese to be hiding in. I had no memory of them as being difficult – but in the expanse of the Essex marshes, things tend to dissolve to brown.

The geese come first as sound. We turn a corner and a muddy channel opens up between two patches of marsh that had earlier appeared seamlessly as one. The wind picks up their calls and the noise drifts over us. It takes me back to a sunburned day last spring, on a clifftop on Orkney, of all places, possibly the very antithesis of here. Brent geese sound oddly, disorientatingly, like gannets. Both have throaty gut-tural calls that sound like heavy, hoarse breathing. Robin Hull's *Scottish Birds: Culture and Tradition* suggests that many of the archaic Scottish names for the brent goose (including the 'rutt goose') are 'deriving from Norse *ratgas* meaning snoring goose.'[3] Each individual note begins as one sound that merges into the cumulative murmurings of the flock.

As I recognise it, I snap out of the brief reverie I'd been lulled into by this nagging and numbing wind.

When we can finally see the flock, they are lurking in the lee of a saltmarsh bank. They are a muddy bird: of muddy places, muddy colour schemes, muddied sounds. They are a shade darker than the marsh, though their colour has no clarity: not really brown or grey but some shade held between the two by black wingtips at one end and a black neck and bill at the other. The only interruption to the black is a white collar on the neck that doesn't meet at the front or the back, the white fraying into black. These are the dark-bellied brent geese of Russia: the darkest of the *Branta* geese, the black geese. *Branta* shares an etymology with 'burnt'. It makes sense.

These brent geese are the perfect birds for the marshes here, and not just because of their colour. Their calls seem to flow through the open spaces. They stand on mud that is treacherous to us, that would let us sink at least up to our thighs. There is not a lot else out there, beyond a redshank that would sometimes turn against the wind, its feathers catching the breeze. The brent geese aren't ruffled.

$$\smile$$

We're feeling pleased that we've found our geese without too much trouble. But this is really only the start of our search. There is a third type of brent goose that can be seen in the country, lurking in plain sight among some of the dark-bellied brent goose flocks of East Anglia: the black brant. Finding it involves an element of luck. They lurk so effectively that I have never seen one before. I try not to twitch* geese – there's a cliché, after all, about chasing wild geese that sums it up.

---

* 'Twitching' is the act of purposefully going to see a rare or unusual bird that has been found by someone else. It is not synonymous with birdwatching.

The black brant is the American brent goose. It looks like a dark-bellied brent if the dark bits were darker, the light bits lighter, and its collar matched at the front of the neck, making it look like a vicar. It is born in Alaska and should spend the winter anywhere along the Pacific coast of America but somehow a few of these, every year, take a wrong turn over the Arctic and join the flock that looks like the next best thing. The marshes by the Naze are home to a flock that had held one periodically over the winter.

The largest flock here is out on Horsey Island, a higher layer of saltmarsh, surrounded by mud and water. Through the telescope, catching enough wind to tremble incessantly, we see a thousand or so brents all standing, heads held high, nervously watching a marsh harrier quartering the rough edges of the marsh. There are adults and young together, the young with pale edges along the neat feathers of their back, creating gently rippling lines.

A pair of rheas are feeding on the farm behind them – two stout grey flightless birds native to South America, their long necks held low, grazing the grass. One raises its head too and assumes the full height of a small person. Surreal, I guess, is the word for it, but it is perfectly real too for Essex and its strange, marshy edge.

More geese fly into the saltmarsh. The vegetation is long and the ground uneven and the flock appears and disappears at whim. Necks held above disappear for minutes at a time when feeding, frustrating our attempts to get a good look. There are a few brents in the flock that appear to be candidates for black brant. Some darker, more contrasting; some with strong neck collars. But telling a brant from a brent is enough of a puzzle when you can see the whole bird, let alone the moving, disappearing fragments of a number of birds. We give up, frustrated, and head back to the car. There are other places, other flocks in which to continue our search for the elusive brant. And despite my frustration, it's still wonderful to have found a new way to explore these familiar landscapes.

It takes over half an hour to drive between Walton-on-the-Naze and Brightlingsea. I had been here before with Miranda on a winter's day when everything was completely different. When the tide was out and the wind was still and our walk was interspersed with the reverberating *whump whump* of military ordnance.

The geese then were clustered in channels, except for two. At first it wasn't clear what was happening. But through binoculars we could see one standing on the breast of another goose on its back in the mud with its wings splayed out and the aggressor's head repeatedly striking at it. The aggressor grabbed the other's head in its bill, and slammed it into the mud. The battered goose lay still. The aggressor waddled off, the apparent perpetrator of attempted murder. The battered goose stirred after a few seconds and shuffled off. This was so far out of character for a brent goose that we were quite disturbed by it, watching out of a morbid, concerned curiosity, witnessing unexplained, unprecedented violence, a goose psychosis. I had not seen a wild goose before – or since – ever behave like this.

The wind was unpleasant at the Naze. At Brightlingsea it is even harsher. We almost decide not to stay. We can't see any geese, even though there should be nowhere for them to hide at high tide, and it's intensely, unpleasantly cold. Dad pushes on anyway. It was the right call.

A kilometre inland along the sea wall and the sun comes out. The river is pushed by the breeze right up to the sea wall. The tips of dead long grasses are just poking out of the waves. And clustering in a dense flock, among the flooded grass stems, are several hundred brent geese, and an almost constant, quietly rolling wave of their calls. We don't spot them until we are close by. And we creep closer. Duck down so as not to stand out on the horizon. Keep our movements slow and steady. And then a jogger runs past. Followed by a cyclist and a dog walker. We realise we look ridiculous, trying to disappear on a sea wall while the world carries on around us. These geese, for whatever reason, don't want to fly, or swim away, or even hold their necks up and look anxiously around like the nervous Naze flocks. They just stay, seeming relaxed. Interested in each other and not us, I sit by the river's edge with my telescope.

Up close brent geese are deceptively small. They are the same length as a mallard, only slightly larger in the wings, or half the size of a Canada goose. They swim past us, grunting, flashing the unexpected colour of a pink tongue. The sun slips out. They turn more brown than grey, a warmer colour than they appeared this morning. On a number of them, the white streaks that break up their brown flanks are thick and bold, and turn their sides paler than their back. Geese are great up close. You can see the individual. But they are great in a flock too, when their shapes become a pattern, but the individual variations: the collar, the shade of the back, the contrast on their flanks, still stand out. They are just brents, no brants, but I don't mind. It is rare to study wild geese up close like this, to be familiar enough to be no enemy.

Essex might appear to be full of peninsulas, fingers of land stretching out into the sea, but I think it's better read the other way: the sea reaching in, leaking water into the flat muddy land, growing eel grass better than arable grass. The estuaries and marshes of the Essex coastline give it a length, at low tide, of 350 miles of treacherous, muddy, marshy land. It was once a smuggler's paradise: now just a brent goose paradise, a vast expanse of food-rich habitat. This very nature, the muddy essence, of the Essex coast makes it ideal for brent geese, more than any other. It also makes it frustrating to navigate. Here at Brightlingsea I have spent the hour looking out over to Mersea Island, just half a mile away at the closest point over the river. It takes forty minutes to drive there, back up the entire tidal limit of the River Colne to the edge of Colchester, the first upstream river crossing. It takes up the majority of the afternoon, but we didn't want to give up the search for a brant. We are dogged and determined despite the wind and the dying light.

Mersea Island is separated from the mainland by more saltmarsh and two creeks that snake around the coast, north and south, to join in the middle. It is exceptionally muddy. From the car park the path winds its way past cottages to the coast. Here the path, hitherto solid, becomes fresh, deep mud, churned to the consistency of soft butter by the many dog walkers. But where there is winter mud in Essex, there are brents. We can see small flocks dotted around as the falling tide reveals yet more mud.

Among dark-bellied brents, a pale-bellied brent stands out. Even in the dying light of the day it is obvious on the far side of the creek, gleaming against its darker cousins, providing the thrill that accompanies any sighting of a creature that is out of place, unexpected. The difference is more obvious than field guides tend to show. Where the black of the neck finishes on the top of the breast, it finishes neatly. A sharp contrast with a light brown breast that is the same colour as the pale flanks.

It has flown a slightly shorter distance, breeding on Svalbard, instead of on the Arctic coast of Russia, but it has overshot its wintering grounds of Denmark and Northumberland and ended further south. Lost geese find the nearest thing to themselves. The pale-bellied brent pretends to keep its cover in the flock, for the safety of numbers. There are only a few thousand geese of this population, and it is regarded by the Joint Nature Conservation Committee as being among the most at-risk goose species in the world.[4] So it might not be the brant we came out here for, but it's an exciting spot nonetheless, justifying our long wintry trek, into the brutal cold wind.

The dying light. We stop walking to watch as dusk sets in and the mud of the creek turns golden, and the avocets in the river go ice blue, the redshank walks on fluorescent legs and grey plovers shuffle darkly, stones brought to life. Skeins of more brent geese score the sky, flying from solid land to seek the shelter of the labyrinth of creeks that comprise the Essex coast.

While we were not seeing black brants in the Essex flocks, we heard the fields at Falkenham in Suffolk had held one. Specifically, in the third field along from the creek. So the next afternoon, here we are. It's another grey day, touched by ice but warmer without the wind. The path we take skirts that field, but the fields are so flat and green that we can see all the way to the edge of Felixstowe. There are no geese to be seen. We decide they must be upriver.

Dad and I drive each other on. It is useful to be searching with someone else, with an equal desire to find a bird that neither of us has seen before. Giving up would be so easy, especially by this point. We've seen plenty of geese already, the weather is dampening my enthusiasm a little, and the likelihood of finding one specific goose doesn't seem promising. Despite all that, we are still longing to catch a glimpse of it. I set off at a quick march down the sea wall and Dad follows. It is flat and straight and the distance deceives. It feels as if we make no progress and the only thing we have seen is a black swan on the river, looking at us looking at it, united by mutual incomprehension. Dad is tiring – less fond of following me as I hack off down sea walls than he once was. There's one merlin on a post, stirring the river's waders and a hare in the field inland. It's not what we came for.

The light is leaching out of the day, the air becoming almost tangible and milky. I might have grown up in Suffolk but sometimes the coast takes on moods where I feel as if I am intruding, where I feel I don't belong. It is doing that now and it sends shivers down my spine. With Dad tiring, we decide to turn back. Half an hour later a large skein of brents flies down the river and lands in the third field, where they are supposed to have been all along. We turn again.

When we reach the field, there are a few hundred brent geese and we both take turns scanning with the telescope, trying to pick out the brant, hoping it's still here. Then, at the back of the flock, I spot it. Maybe. It is intently grazing, mostly with its back turned to us. It looks darker but that is not enough. It takes a few, tense minutes, my eye not leaving the telescope eyepiece, for it to turn. And when it does, the flanks are almost white. The back is a dark black and so is the breast. Together they are almost the same black as the neck. The neck collar meets at the front, like a pearly white, expensive smile. It carries a clarity about it. A sharper goose. Triumphantly I take a terrible photograph with my phone pressed to the telescope.

Later I send that photo of a distant brant with brents to Laurie and Katie, a pair of friends who have an interest in birds. The first time I met them we ended up talking brants, and how they were convinced that they didn't exist. I thought this was nicely circular in our friendship but instead they're still not convinced of the differences. Katie asks, 'If you can't tell, why does it matter?'

Slightly deflated, I'm not sure how to answer that.

5

White-fronted Geese

Why does it matter that it was a brant and not a brent? Why should I care for the minuteness of this difference? Perhaps it is the understanding of feeling a bit different that underpins this for me.

I grew up awkward. Always uncertain of my place in the scheme of things. Never sure what I was working towards. The world was vast and perplexing and the temptation to retreat into books was always strong. Getting into nature – in the broadest sense of the world around me – was a salve. It did not save me from awkwardness or solve me. But it helped me begin to understand the world. Nature seems to come loaded with a seriousness that was attractive to me as a serious, po-faced teenager, yearning to know more about the world and my place in it. It seemed easier than knowing my place in the shifting sands of school social groups.

So these differences seem important to me. It feels like an act of empathy. On one level it does not really matter at all: brants and brents are the same species. But 'species' is a vague concept; it is similar to the diffuse border between a language and a dialect. If each species is a language, it comes with a range of dialects and accents, each as valid and worthy of recognition as any other. To me, the same is true of geese. Each species is unique, has its own unique habits, no matter how similar they might at first appear. But we can go further. Each name we give to each type of goose is a hook on which to hang more interest, more discoveries – all of which adds more to our knowledge of birds.

Nature is serious. But it is also ridiculous. Take geese: a sort of mega duck that goes *honk* and flies from Britain to the furthest point north where there is land, to places that live on the edge of my imagination, ushering the winter in and out. The more I learn, the more I know about nature's constituent parts, the more ridiculous joy it gives me: a ridiculous man who likes looking at birds and will travel across the country to look at some more. All because of the minute differences in feathers that make up the physical appearance of a goose. This quest becomes something bigger. A way of understanding the world around me. A way of understanding me.

Late last year, David Borthwick had taken me into old Galloway, to the RSPB reserve at the Ken-Dee marshes on a day deep in December gloom, the horizon shrouded in a drizzle that was coming and going in waves. In the foreground a pair of belted Galloways, a local breed of cow with deceptively short legs that gave the impression that they were sinking into the damp, dank, black mud. The day was sinking into itself, subsiding in its own bleakness. Greenland white-fronted geese roost on the loch and feed in the fields here.

Just because Greenland white-fronts are supposed to be here doesn't mean they always are. That day it was empty of geese. We scrabbled around for what we could find instead. Just one red squirrel, a procession of blue tits and great tits to the peanut feeder, and two red-kite-shaped smudges sitting in the distant trees, whistling mournfully in the drizzle. Frustrated at the lack of activity, sitting in the hide with not much to see, I checked a local wildlife group on Facebook and saw pictures of the Greenland white-fronts and felt a rare pang of jealousy.

Like brents, the white-fronted goose is globally common, or in the language of the conservation lists, 'of least concern'. The species breeds across the Arctic, but there are subtle differences between the populations that breed in Greenland and those that breed in Russia. The Russian-born birds have a distinctive white forehead, back from a pink bill. Their bodies are uniform grey-brown, slightly lighter only at the breast, and white behind the legs to the tail. Their bellies have a variable black barring, a few token tiger stripes, different on every individual bird. Those that breed in Greenland are slightly larger, the feathers darker. Their bills are longer and orange, instead of pink, though the two are still surprisingly similar and difficult to tell apart. The difference was noticed and written up for the scientific record by Peter Scott only in 1948, and even he wasn't convinced it was overly important.[1]

I disagree. These are different birds, however similar they may appear, and they are unique. Of all the grey geese, the Greenland white-front stands out from the others. We know that they stay together as families for longer than other *Anser* geese – up to nine winters has been recorded for certain individuals. This is interesting because it suggests that learned behaviours have developed within the family groups.[2] The Greenland white-front is also the only goose that breeds in the Arctic that undertakes two separate legs of its migration, both challenging and arduous routes covering more than a thousand kilometres.[3] For adult Greenland white-fronted geese that migrate across the Atlantic Ocean and then the Greenland ice cap, the annual survival rate – when there is no hunting – is 89 per cent.[4] This is an astonishing feat of endurance and persistence over distance and inhospitable terrain. In comparison, for barnacle geese that make the migration from the Netherlands to Novaya Zemlya, the annual survival rate is 55 per cent.[5]

These birds are worthy of our recognition and it is only by recognising their differences that we can keep track of them – and take notice when a population is in decline.

⌣

There are two types of rarity and two types of decline. In Britain, the Russian white-fronted geese are quite rare, only here briefly and not at many regular sites, although they're the ones I am most familiar with as a few flocks winter in Suffolk. But there are no internationally important flocks of them. Across my lifetime they have declined by 69 per cent.[6] Now only 2,100 spend the winter here.[7] But this is not really a cause for concern. Their global numbers aren't in decline; they're just finding somewhere else to spend the winter, closer to home as conditions there improve for them.[8]

In Britain the Greenland white-fronted goose is much more common: averaging 12,000 wintering here, mostly along the west coast of Scotland, fewer in Wales, and an irregular handful in England. There's another 11,000 in the Republic of Ireland. But despite these numbers being higher than those for the Russian birds, this is a third less Greenland white-fronted geese than were here in 2003, and that is worrying. That this constitutes the entire population of Greenland white-fronted geese is exceptionally worrying. The WWT picks them out as one of the most at-risk goose species in the UK.[9] Their decline here is not because of improvement elsewhere: there is nowhere else for them to go, no land between Greenland and here for them to winter. Their population is simply dwindling. And even here it is sometimes a struggle to maintain a place for them.

Greenland white-fronted geese have a preference for spending winter nights roosting on peat bogs up the west coast of Scotland. In the mid 1980s there was a fight over the role of Duich Moss (Eilean na Muice Duibhe) on the island of Islay. United Malt and Grain Distillers Ltd wanted to cut the peat for use in whisky production, where drying malt over peat fire gives the whisky of Islay its distinctive smoky flavour.

But the European Commission intervened: Duich Moss held an internationally significant roost of Greenland white-fronts, and under European law it should have been protected, despite the decision to cut the peat having been approved by British politicians. It worked: saved by Europe, Duich Moss was ratified as a Special Protection Area and a Ramsar site – an international level of protection for wetland – in 1988. The distillers found an alternative source of peat. The geese kept their nightly home. It is a great example. It shows how conservation works best when it transcends national borders that mean little to migratory birds anyway.

The decline in numbers is still a worry. Loss of habitat is definitely a concern, but another culprit is hunting. These are geese that are born to survive – shown by their remarkable survival rate over an incredibly tough migratory path – but these white-fronts have no surplus to lose. A study into hunting at Wexford Slobs – a wetland in the southeastern corner of the Republic of Ireland, where almost half the world's population spends the winter – found that the birds that were shot would not have died from other causes such as predation or lack of food.[10] They were needed to sustain the population. This was borne out when, after the hunting stopped, the population grew by 4 per cent each year.[11] The report also states that on the Dyfi estuary in Wales it was only a long-running voluntary moratorium on shooting, dating back to 1972, that prevented the flock's extinction there.[12] A bill was finally drawn up in November 2018, proposing to enshrine this into law, bringing England and Wales – the last places where they could be hunted – in line with every other country that is home to Greenland white-fronted geese.

To many of us, preventing the hunting of geese to save them might seem a small cultural sacrifice. But they have been hunted for a very long time, and it's proving a hard habit to break. The earliest white-fronted goose that I can find dates from four millennia ago. In the art of Ancient Egypt, we can see wildfowling scenes, painted with exceptional clarity. They show hunters throwing sticks, setting clap nets and using (presumably trained) cats.* In *Nebamun Hunting in the Marshes* the hunter's cat leaps after a waterbird that I can't identify. A few birds above the cat's outstretched paw, fleeing with a tangible terror, is a waterbird with wings open and flapping, and a few bars on the breast, unlike any other species.

---

* How one trains a cat to catch a goose and bring it back is unknown to me.

There has always been an open season on geese, ever since Nebamun and his cat. The British Association of Shooting and Conservation lobbied against the outlawing of hunting Greenland white-fronted geese, preferring instead a voluntary moratorium. The Russian population can be legally hunted in seventeen European countries. The numbers killed have increased by 579 per cent in the past decade: from 2,209 to 15,003 individual birds.[13] They are not listed as a species of concern – yet. But who knows what effect such an increase might have in the future. When Peter Scott first saw the flock of Russian white-fronted geese that winter on the Severn estuary, in 1945, he 'had a most wonderful view of a great flock of 2,000 wild geese'.[14] That flock is now the size of all the Russian-bred white-fronts that spend the winter here in Britain.

There was another species in the flock of white-fronts that Peter Scott saw. To be accurate, all the white-fronted geese I have written about so far have been greater white-fronted geese. The lesser white-fronted goose is another species, one that only very rarely finds itself among a flock of the wrong species, migrating to the wrong country. They are almost identical to greater white-fronted geese: the differences are subtle and require a close view, a good light and ideally a greater white-fronted goose to serve as a comparison. They are also the species that Scandinavian conservationists have recognised as being extremely vulnerable to extinction.

They are the smallest of all the grey geese,[15] but only just. Their heads are smaller and their beaks thinner and pointier: cumulatively they look smaller than they are. On the adults, the white blaze behind the bill runs further up the forehead, touching the crown of the head. The eye is ringed with gold, like a gilt edge, although this is thin and difficult to see from a distance. That is pretty much the only feature distinguishing it from the greater white-fronted goose.

A small irony is that they breed much closer to Britain than greater white-fronted geese, in the taiga forests of Arctic Norway and Finland. But instead of tracking west on their winter migration, like the Russian-born greater white-fronted geese, they head straight south, pausing in the Hortobágy of Hungary, before carrying on to the wetlands of Bulgaria and northern Greece. Here they overlap with other species, including greater white-fronted geese, which is a risk. When lurking among birds that can be hunted legally and that are almost indistinguishable from them, they are easily shot by mistake.

In response to its threatened status, there are projects to reintroduce the bird to the wild across Europe. One such project is in Sweden, run by the Jägareförbundet (the Swedish Association for Hunting and Wildlife Management). It attempted, successfully, to forge a new wintering area for the geese by releasing young lesser white-fronts that had grown up with barnacle geese 'foster parents'. As geese migrate in their family groups, the young lesser white-fronts are shown the barnacle goose's migratory route, which takes them into the Netherlands, a place the species had never wintered before, but safely away from areas where they might be hunted. It reminds me of a sentimental film I watched as a child, *Fly Away Home*, in which a flock of Canada geese is guided on their migration from Ontario to North Carolina by a girl and her father flying a microlight aircraft. A report by Sovon, the Dutch Centre for Field Ornithology, says that by 2013 there was a wintering population of 130 individuals in the Netherlands – and that the majority of them are Swedish reintroduced birds.[16]

Despite its success, the project has proved controversial with Norwegian conservationists, who have raised concerns over hybridisation between lesser white-fronted geese and barnacle geese, which would not happen in the wild, and the choosing of 'undesired' stopover sites in migration such as city parks.[17] Perhaps these foster parents, chosen only for their migration path, aren't the ideal species for the role.[18] However, a Finnish scheme to reintroduce lesser white-fronted geese did not use foster parents and was unsuccessful – none of the released birds bred and at least seven were shot.[19] Although we don't, and possibly can't, know if the lack of foster parents was related to the failure, it seems likely that it was.

The differences of opinion are mostly philosophical. At the heart of it seems to be the dilemma – or the choice – of what we want nature to be: as untouched and self-willed as possible, or whether, in the modern world, it is necessary to meddle as much as we do. Those involved in the Swedish project consider it more important to ensure the survival of the population in Sweden, by whatever means necessary.[20] In an article for the *Harrier*, Suffolk birder Richard Attenborrow commented that for the opposition the attitude seemed to be 'better to be natural and dead'.[21]

The scheme reminds me of Scott and the early days of the WWT in its judicious use of captive rearing to supplement populations at risk, and the way that hunters are proactively trying to assist with wildlife populations. Despite our many attempts at interfering with nature, I can't think of a precedent for a species where humans have wilfully altered its distribution range with the aim of saving the species.

In 2015 four of the project's young lesser white-fronted geese, one with a satellite tag, overshot on migration, turning up at the RSPB's Minsmere reserve on the Suffolk coast. The four spent the night there without being seen before the tagged bird's position was noticed on the satellite map. They were first identified by human eyes the next day at North Warren, before they toured Hazelwood Marshes and Sudbourne Marshes, a triangle of good goose-feeding on the coast before they headed to Belgium after three days in Suffolk.

When they were at North Warren, they were with 160 greater white-fronted geese and 20 tundra bean geese. I was lucky to catch them during their brief stay. Even without my current interest in geese I was aware of what a remarkable sighting this was. Rare birds tangled up with conservation in action – the idea was thrilling. I stared at them through my telescope, a distant smorgasbord of good geese on a day when the January sun was hazing the marsh. The lesser white-fronts were dark and distant and noticeably small and neatly proportioned. Their bills were short and seemed as if they'd been pushed into the birds' heads, which were squarer shaped than the other species. One of the flock had a thin black line, curving out from the feathers of its back – the satellite tag that meant we knew exactly where it was and where it had been and where it would go, and where it had originated: it was the offspring of an adult caught breeding in Russia, north of the Ural mountains.[22]

North Warren was the first place I ever went birding by myself, one frigid December day, as a fourteen-year-old. It was cold, muddy and I lacked confidence in all my identifications. I took it as an excuse to eat lots of chocolate. It was great. Subsequently I went every winter while I lived in Suffolk. I remember it now more as a place, rather than for great birding. Each time I reacquainted myself with what I really remembered North Warren for: the quality of its mud. North Warren has two marshes, one north and one south of a causeway. No matter what the weather was that winter, it always felt as if the causeway was a bank of pure mud. Walkers and birders would churn it daily and you could either slip with every step, or stick, the path sucking at your boots, clumping around the soles and weighing down your ankles. And it was not without risks: there were reeds, brambles and ditches each side of the path if you slipped too far. And if I was carrying Dad's telescope, I would try to save that first. A broken leg should mend; borrowed optical equipment breaks expensively.

It was on winter days like those that my love of Suffolk, my love of home, was hatched, to the point that any marsh, any low expanse of wet grass and reed-lined ditches anywhere in the world now feels like home. It was on those birding trips – typic-ally Sunday afternoons, homework always waiting for another day – that formed my idea of winter, what I think about when I think about the season. A time of pale-blue skies, golden reeds and good birds to be found. I loved it then and I still think I do, when not submerged in tepid grey for days on end.

Still down in Suffolk, I'm keen to revisit the place that holds such memories, so Dad and I return to North Warren. I don't expect it to be as generous with its geese as last time, although I still secretly hope.

Overnight Suffolk remains frozen. We have woken up to a dawn dappled pink behind the black fretwork of the oak trees. Dad points the car down the winding road out of the village, briefly crossing the plains of the sugar-beet fields, iced as though they are tundra. The sun feels in that moment as if it has the warmth of the first sunrise after the gloom of an Arctic winter. It is apricot, egg yolk, tangerine, clouds blushing pink and a cold blue sky peeking through. Even though by the time we reach the coast, the sun has passed into grey again, it is enough.

I had never seen ice on a beach. The shingle solid, each individual pebble delicately thorned with the hoar frost. The night evidently was bitter enough to defeat the salty coastal atmosphere that resists ice and frost. The causeway mud is frozen solid: a blessing, to walk here without sliding or clumped mud weighing our boots down. I stop at the last bush, using it to hide my body from wary geese. The marsh is bleached with ice. I scan to the far corner where the geese usually are. There are none. Fleetingly my heart sinks – the frost must have forced them off, moved the geese towards open water or better feeding. And then I put my binoculars down, and realise they're right in front me. Relief.

I count forty-one greater white-fronted geese. Russian birds, as they should be here, bills as pink as my cold nose, in a flock of more barnacle geese. I have never seen wild geese in this corner of the marsh before. The white-fronts are wary, warier than the barnacle geese, but the need for food overrides that. Through the telescope we watch them, intently. One, at least, always seems to be watching us back.

They graze with neat gestures, making small move-ments with their heads, always shuffling forwards. With their heads held low, the frozen grass hiding their distinctive white foreheads, it falls to the black stripes of the adult's belly to mark them out. It is startling to see them to so close. I zoom out with the telescope and scan across the middle ground of the marsh, and find ninety-eight more lurking in plain sight, sporadically hiding among the greylag geese.

They are pretty for a grey goose: neat, compact and elegant in shape. Their plumage is cleaner-cut than the other *Ansers*, the stripes and white fore-head aesthetically pleasing. It all feels right with the marsh, crisp and haloed in frost, reflecting the clear air.

We walk on after a while, aiming for the far cor-ner of the marsh, where the geese usually are, but it's empty today. The cold has scattered them across the marsh instead. A sparrowhawk glides along the line of reeds and settles on a gate – bright-eyed and glaring in the grey. In the next field a fox burns bright against the frost, in a field with lapwings and a curlew uttering a three-note alarm call. It marks its territory – as it had on the path with its distinctive smell, like cheap cigarettes – and disappears into the hedge.

It's time to move on, we have a new place to be. One more goose to find before I must head back home to Scotland.

6

Bean Geese

There is less than two miles between North Warren and Aldeburgh town marsh, but they feel completely different. The frozen clarity has been replaced by grey. A murkiness is setting in and sleet is beginning to fall from the clouds as we park the car between the beach and the marsh. The sky is flat, featureless silver grey and the sea is grey, gently rippling. The river is between its tidal extremes. The mud shines but reflects nothing. The river water goes nowhere. Beyond, the masts of the mysterious installations of Orford Ness are retreating into the dim mist.

Aldeburgh town marsh stretches inland, fading out into the murk. It is laid out before us and we can see all it seems to hold. Or doesn't hold, as seems to be the case right now. There are supposed to be four tundra bean geese here, but instead we have the bleak prospect of an empty marsh. North Warren was the promised land, some avian Eden, compared to this marsh of nothing but pale stripes of brown reeds and green grass and muddy tedium. And I'm aware that my time down here is fast drawing to a close.

Eventually we come to a bend in the river, a gate and some birds, tucked along the bank, no longer obscured. There are four swans sitting down. A small flock of brent geese that I scan through, the habit of looking for brants now ingrained. There are no brant but by this point just finding some geese, any geese, to look at feels like a success. Through the wider view of binoculars, I pick out six other geese, asleep. Two are large, uniformly grey-brown, greylag geese. Four are smaller. Pink-footed geese, I think, and carry on searching, scanning behind all the tufts of longer grass and lines of reeds. Dad thinks they're worth another look. I don't.

Dad says, 'I'm pretty sure they might be the tundras.'

Confident I saw pink-legs, I carry on searching.

'They're awake now.'

I carry on searching.

'I think they have orange legs.'

I spin the telescope around just in time to see the goose sit down, hiding its legs. I think the bill might be orange. It is hard to tell, peering into the murk, where the border of pink ends and orange begins. These colours seem easy to define until you need to, on a distant bird, a small speck. It goes to sleep, bill tucked under wing. Another one wakes up. Unfurls its neck, untucking its head. Dark head, dark bill with a flash of, again, I think, orange. It stands up on incontrovertibly orange legs, luminous in the murk.

A bean goose. Our run of luck continues. The last of our wild wintering geese species seen.

There are two types of bean goose in Britain (of five globally): tundra and taiga. They are the most challenging geese to tell apart. The differences are present but not always evident. Or agreed upon. David Cabot's *Wildfowl* is a sober book, yet when he begins his account of the bean goose in Britain and Ireland, there's a palpable stress caused by the species: 'The bean goose, a taxonomic nightmare with disagreement among experts on the number of its subspecies/species, is closely related to the pink-footed goose – which itself has been classified by some ornithologists as a subspecies of the bean goose.'[1]

The basic bean goose is, at first glance, a copy of the pink-footed goose. The pattern is the same. Dark head, brown body, white behind the legs to the tail.

It differs in its orange rather than pink legs and bill, and it doesn't have the greyish cast to the back.

Part of the taxonomic nightmare is down to the similarity of appearance, but there are differences. While tundra beans are the same size and shape as pink-footed geese, taiga beans are larger, and the bill is longer, usually with more orange in it. The tundra beans also have a stubbier, darker bill.

This species – or should that be these species? – is like the Russian white-fronted goose, in that it has a large European population, but is at the very edge of its wintering range here in Britain, and present in even lower numbers. Only about 200 taiga bean geese winter here, split into two populations: an English and a Scottish flock. Even fewer tundra bean geese winter here, just 100, though illogically they are easier to see because they are nomads. They turn up in flocks of the other species, or just by themselves, spread throughout the goose regions of the country.

As the name suggests, the taiga beans breed in the taiga forests of Scandinavia.* The tundra bean geese breed further north, beyond the trees, across a swathe of northern Siberia. The other part of their name stems from old wintering habits: beans would have been part of their diet. It was also once known as the 'corn goose'.[2] Nowadays, like most geese, they would probably be named the 'marsh grass goose'.

These Aldeburgh bean geese have the basic pattern of a pink-foot. But the back is plain dark without the grey cast. The bill has limited orange but more importantly is short. They owe more to the pink-foot than the greylag in stature. They are, by process of elimination – the algorithm of plumage and structure – tundra and not taiga.

For some reason I'm not as excited by the discovery as I ought to be. I think it's the weather. Although

---

* Taiga forests are the conifer forests of the far north of Scandinavia, Russia and North America (where they are known as boreal forests).

the connection between these birds and the winter landscape usually delights me, with the sleet beginning, and the cold setting in, these four tundra beans by themselves, distant and mostly sleeping, seem a tad underwhelming. So we retreat.

The next day is the warmest forecast in East Anglia but it feels like the coldest. The murk of dawn resolved into more murk. The bulk of Norfolk hanging onto darkness. As the sun rises along the roads, the mist does not shift but clings, assisted by rain showers, and even inside the heated car involuntary shivers pass through me, as if my eyes are conducting the cold straight through the windscreen to the marrow of my bones.

Today we're heading to the Yare valley, where the marshes hold the English flock of taiga bean geese – the only place to have taiga bean geese in

England every year, thanks to the magic combination of wet grassland, ditches and mud: food and shelter. Although that doesn't mean we'll be able to see them today. In the late 1980s and early 1990s the Yare flock reached almost 500 birds. In the winter of 2017–18 that was down to eighteen birds.

We know an unusual amount about the Yare flock of taiga bean geese, partly due to the efforts of Mariko Parslow-Otsu in tagging and tracking birds, and partly because geese are creatures of habit. We know that those that spend the winter by the Yare are birds that breed in central Sweden and mostly spend the winter in the northwest of Denmark, a number of whom go on to cross the North Sea, and head southwest to mid-Norfolk.[3] As with the decline in Russian-born white-fronted geese, the WWT believes this is due to short-stopping: the milder winters of north and west Europe mean the taiga beans are staying in Denmark instead of carrying on with the risks of migration. The conditions in

Denmark are improving for them, while those here seem to be getting worse.

We start at Cantley Marshes. The track is lined by reeds, and wooden gates onto the marsh become our viewpoints, revealing wet grassy fields and the horizon of a pale grey ring of trees through mist and rain. And not a lot else. The ditches are frozen fast and reflect white sky. Puddles on the path and fallen reeds are encased in ice. Through the gloom we can find only one pink-footed goose, by itself, lurking in a patch of longer grass. It might be injured, or ill: it is unusual to see a social animal like a goose by itself, vulnerable. The likelihood is that it clipped a power line nearby, damaging a wing, leaving it unable to fly with the rest of the flock. Or maybe this one lost its partner and had no young. Maybe it just fell out of the social system. Maybe it was a loner and wanted to be this way. The individual lives and thoughts of birds are something I desire to know and doubt I ever can.

I'm keen to avoid the disappointing anticlimax of yesterday's find. So far, birds are obvious by their absence: only a little egret as white as the sky, a couple of herons as grey as the horizon, and a kestrel sitting damply in a tree. But never mind. Finding birds on these marshes, in a landscape so big and full of places to hide, is like a card game. We debate whether to stick or twist. We choose to twist.

A few miles upriver lie Buckenham Marshes, an unbroken chain of ditch-lined green marshes. It should be goose heaven: a paradise of grazing and space and a horizon for the wary. There is no way anything could sneak up on a goose here; their long necks snaking up over the vegetation around them, heads turning, eyes scanning the surroundings. I did not come here expecting good views. But I did come here expecting to see something. At least *some* geese. The winter landscape seems incomplete now without them in it.

It is approaching midday. The shroud of mist shows no sign of lifting. All we've seen at Buckenham is wigeon. Thousands of wigeon. It would be possible to believe that wigeon are the only birds left on earth. They spook – I don't know why, I can see no reason – and fling themselves up and circle around as a tight flock, like a murmuration of starlings, around me. They whistle. A sound that is joyous and echoes around the mist-bound marsh.

Maybe I'm not focused enough to find bean geese today. My concentration keeps wandering off into cul-de-sacs of daftness, into a world of wigeon. Even when methodically searching with the telescope, I get distracted by workers on the railway in high-vis orange suits, half a mile away. Their colours are startling in the murk that stretches the distance.

Suddenly there is the sound of geese – pink-feet – flying into the far corner of the marsh, over near the railway line, their calling carrying through the distance and the murk. It works like an adrenaline shot. My meandering mind snaps to attention. My eye focuses in. J. A. Baker wrote of how his 'eye becomes insatiable for hawks. It clicks towards towards them with ecstatic fury.'[4] I do that with geese now.

At half a mile a goose is not a big bird – it's a blemish, a small dark smudge, its colours faded through the mist and rain. In a flock where one of the most useful distinguishing features – leg colour – can't be seen behind a patch of long grass, it becomes significantly more difficult to pick out the rare smudge that might be a taiga bean goose.

Finally – apart from the main flock, there's one that fits, that fulfils the ID criteria even at this range. A bigger, darker goose. It has orange legs, almost the same colour as the high-vis jackets of the railway workers. The bill is muddy – colourless but big.

Success. Perhaps again the effort has outweighed the reward – a rather distant, indistinct goose. It would be OK to think that after three long walks through repetitive, empty landscapes in unpleasant weather. But not for me: doggedness has a way of justifying itself and it would have been worse not to find it at all after that. It feels good that we have almost been outwitted by the wiliest and rarest of wintering geese, in a landscape that belongs to it and not to us.

We are heading to Holkham, the final stop on my goose-finding tour. I'm hoping to finish on a high. The north Norfolk coast is a crown of mud and sand, water and grass. It is jewelled with nature reserves, enough for it to be a birder's playground. Holkham might be the biggest jewel. The best patchwork of habitats. The widest sweep of space. Conditions here are just right for a large amount of geese.

That also means a large amount of people and it is slightly jarring to go from the emptiness of the

Yare valley – where we saw one other birdwatcher, one dog walker and the railway workers – to the car park at Holkham, with its long string of well-washed 4×4 cars and obedient Labradors waiting to be let off their leads at the beach.

We get out of the car and it is sunny, the light limpid and sparkling across the marsh for several miles east and west. I can see, instantly, a flock of pink-feet containing more geese than I saw this morning, and this flock is small only for here. There will be, I suspect, plenty more spread out for miles around me.

There are supposed to be two tundra bean geese out here, mixed in with the pink-feet. As far as I can tell they aren't in the flock in front of me, though it is hard to be certain with a number of the flock asleep, or lurking behind reeds. I walk on, certain of finding more. And I do see a handful of white-fronted geese and pink-feet and greylags but nothing resembling a tundra bean. The marsh here is a raptor's paradise. A peregrine falcon buzzes along the line of pine trees, banks and heads out over the marsh, disappearing into the distance in the blink of an eye. Kestrels and marsh harriers fly more slowly, more leisurely, with less absolute intent, and a buzzard sits on top of a bush with even less intent. A few thousand more wigeon are out there too.

The tundra bean geese remain elusive. And my time is up. I'm not as disappointed as I thought, find myself looking forward to future winters, future expeditions. There will be plenty of other chances for me to find them. After all, these particular geese are creatures of habit, always faithfully returning here.

I envy the geese their certainty, their habits of home. I am forever torn between multiple places that feel like home. Scotland where I live or Suffolk, Essex, Norfolk: the flatlands of golden evenings and reeds, mud and water and sand. The distant horizon and all the space in between I grew up with, which seems to lurk somewhere, subconsciously calling me back.

⌣

It feels good to be back in Scotland. Back to the regular passing of pink-feet over the quiet edges of Dumfries. I cast glances at maps of the Scottish taiga bean goose flock, and the Slamannan Plateau between the towns of Falkirk and Cumbernauld, where they winter on the patchwork of fields, moor and loch. It's too far. I have travelled enough. I am exhausted by running around after bean geese.

February comes with a heatwave. February comes with the rude awakening of butterflies from their winter torpor, wings roused by unexpected, unseasonal heat. I take a break. I walk down the river, not seeing any butterflies (unlike Miranda, who today over near Kirkcudbright sees a butterfly and a day-flying bat). I am weak: easily led to enjoy an unseasonal burst of warmth after the winter, by the sheer joy of sun on skin, even though I know this is bad, that this is a sign of global warming and the Anthropocene and the awful shifting of the patterns and systems with which wildlife evolved. Because winter here should be cold. And it has been cold and wet and home to geese for a very long period of time.

In the past I wouldn't have needed to go so far, to either Slamannan or the Yare valley, to find a taiga bean goose. I could have taken a bus the short distance west from Dumfries to Castle Douglas, and found them on the Dee marshes, where for sixty years they wintered in flocks of up to 500, before a slow decline turned into a steady dissipation.

One of the problems is that they were, in the nineteenth century, thought to be one of the commonest grey geese in Scotland, but this was a time where we weren't aware of all the distinctions between the different species and all wild grey geese were assumed to be bean.[5] When Gladstone wrote his entry for bean geese in *The Birds of Dumfriesshire* he quoted from Thomas Aird's poem, *A Winter's Day*: 'The wild geese cackled through the firmament, / Far going down upon the softer south: / These be the tokens of a rigorous time.'[6] It seems obvious now that these might all have been misidentified pink-feet.

In any case, the taiga haven't wintered there since the 1980s. From the 1950s the record books reveal ephemeral flocks: Loch Lomond, Loch of Strathbeg, Slains Loch, the Carron Valley Reservoir.[7] Their story was always the same. Turning up, wintering, moving on after a few seasons, in search of somewhere else, always elusive, hard to know. We don't really know why. They are the ultimate elusive wild goose, the very opposite of our semi-tame park geese.

My penultimate goose flew over the high street just after dusk. The street was empty – Dumfries has its ghost-town moments – and the *wink wink* of several pink-footed geese unseen against the dark sky echoed off the sandstone buildings and glass shopfronts. I didn't know if it would be the end. A week later a chiffchaff sings from the park, its two-note name the song it uses to herald spring in the weak sunshine. There's a warmth to the air. Sand martins over the river, and grey wagtails flashing their streak of luminous yellow as they pirouette, picking off the stoneflies emerging from the riverbed. The water is low and clear, rippling over the stony floor, unlike the thick, ominous brown flow of the winter spate. There are daffodils, coltsfoot, cuckooflower. And the sheer shock of a peacock butterfly's wing: burgundy and sky blue, a golden eye on each wing watching the watcher. The vividness of the new season. The shock of spring.

Not all the geese leave at the same time. Some cling on at the Solway marshes until late spring.

These might be just young birds reluctant about returning, injured birds that can't, or adults that won't breed. But with the changing of the season they begin to feel out of place. Wild geese and warmth is an odd combination for Dumfries. But I am pleased their departure wasn't a rupture: a sudden absence of geese but something more gradual that suits the segueing of the seasons.

Absence is hard to notice – like the realisation one late summer's day when the streets are suddenly silent and the swifts have gone; it is startling and briefly saddening. There is no chance to say goodbye and the absence feels almost keener for it. For several days I scan the sky and listen out eagerly, waiting to watch and acknowledge and wish farewell for the season to any flock I see.

My last Dumfries goose was on 10 April. A small skein of ten pink-feet, low in the mid-afternoon. I was in the park, in my shirtsleeves, I could have been wearing shorts, and the sky was a stunning blue. The skein turned northeast over the town. I go online later and see an observer on the Isle of Skye has noticed big flocks moving north throughout the day. Not an exodus but a return, as they follow the fleeing winter. And it is unusual – low enough, late enough and loud enough to be obvious, to stand out. I nod my head at them. Wish them the best. And hope to see them in the last week of next September, with their new young in the skein, wintering again.

Acknowledgements

Thanks to Jennie Condell and Pippa Crane for their superb editing and belief in me as a writer, and for not laughing out loud when the idea for this book landed in their inboxes. And my thanks and gratitude to the rest of the team at E&T. Dan Mogford did the brilliant cover, the copyeditor was Jill Burrows and the proofreader was James Rose.

This book was born out of a specific time and place. So it feels right to acknowledge and offer my biggest thanks to Miranda Cichy, who was the driving force behind the move to Dumfries while I was wrapped up in finishing *The Seafarers*. All the DIY I can do won't be enough to pay off that debt. As with *The Seafarers* every sentence was dissected and criticised by Miranda and Victoria Cichy. Thanks to

Morag, our cat, for sitting on my hands and reminding me that it is OK to take a break.

Dr David Borthwick deserves special thanks as well for gracefully tolerating my presence on his intellectual patch, and for being exceptionally generous with resources, stimulating conversation, trips to Caerlaverock and Mersehead and for his infectious goose enthusiasm.

For Abigail Cheverst, Oliver Bothwell and Jake Hearn: thank you, because all three of you thought you were coming for a nice weekend away in Scotland, and instead you got copious rain and even more unexpected geese. Thanks also to Laurie and Katie Handcock for putting up with my brant rants; to Eddie Bathgate, Kane Brides, Gi Grieco and Larry Griffin for their assistance with answering goose questions; to Lev Parikian for having an opinion on the best way to describe Jean Sibelius; and to the staff at the Ewart Library in Dumfries for putting up with me constantly wanting books out of your basement.

Acknowledgements

To everyone we know in Dumfries, thank you for your warmth which helped make us feel so welcome. Thanks to the WWT and the RSPB for running the wonderful Caerlaverock and Mersehead reserves that are so important for the barnacle goose.

This book is for my parents. Thanks for everything.

And thanks to the geese themselves, for keeping winter bearable since the Pleistocene.

Bibliography

Armstrong, Edward A., *The Folklore of Birds* (London: Collins, 1958)

Attenborrow, Richard, 'Lesser white-fronted goose – revisited', *The Harrier* (195) Winter 2018, pp. 10–11

Baker, J. A., *The Peregrine* (New York: New York Review of Books, 2005)

Birkhead, Tim, et al., *Ten Thousand Birds: Ornithology since Darwin* (Princeton: Princeton University Press, 2014)

Borthwick, David, 'Innsidh Na Geòidh As T-Fhoghar E: the geese will tell it in the autumn', *EarthLines* (November 2015), pp. 52–7

Brides, Kane; Carl Mitchell, et al., *Status and distribution of Icelandic-breeding geese: results of the 2017 international census* (Slimbridge: Wildfowl and Wetlands Trust, 2018)

Cabot, David, *Wildfowl* (London: Collins, 2009)

Cocker, Mark and Richard Mabey, *Birds Britannica* (London: Chatto & Windus, 2005)

Defoe, Daniel, *A Tour Through the Whole Island of Great Britain* (London: Penguin, 1976)

Forrester, R. W.; I. J. Andrews, et al., *The Birds of Scotland: Volume 1* (Aberlady: The Scottish Ornithologists' Club, 2007)

Francis, Ian, 'A drain on geese', *Geographical Magazine* (November, 1986)

Frost, Teresa, et al., 'Population estimates of wintering waterbirds in Great Britain', *British Birds* (112) March 2019, pp. 130–45

Gallico, Paul, *The Snow Goose* (London: Penguin, 1967)

Gerald of Wales, *The History and Topography of Ireland*, trans. by John O'Meara (London: Penguin, 1982)

Gladstone, Hugh S., *The Birds of Dumfriesshire* (London: Witherby & Co, 1910)

Goss, Glenda Dawn, *Sibelius: A Composer's Life and the Awakening of Finland* (Chicago: University of Chicago Press, 2009)

Grant, John, 'A wild goose chase with a difference', *The Harrier* (180) Spring 2015, pp. 7–8

Hirschfeld, Axel; Geraldine Attard, et al., 'Bird hunting in Europe: an analysis of bag figures and the potential

impact on the conservation of threatened species',
British Birds (112), March 2019, pp. 153–66

Hull, Robin, *Scottish Birds: Culture and Tradition*
(Edinburgh: Mercat Press, 2001)

Lankester, Sir Ray, *Diversions of a Naturalist* (London:
Methuen & Co., 1915)

Leopold, Aldo, *A Sand County Almanac* (Oxford:
Oxford University Press, 1968)

Leopold, Aldo, *Round River: From the Journals of
Aldo Leopold* (Oxford: Oxford University Press,
1993)

Mynott, Jeremy, *Birds in the Ancient World* (Oxford:
Oxford University Press, 2018)

Mynott, Jeremy, *Birdscapes: Birds in Our Imagination
and Experiences* (Princeton: Princeton University
Press, 2009)

Percival, Steve and Eric Bignal, 'The Islay barnacle goose
management strategy: A suggested way forward',
British Wildlife (October 2018), pp. 37–44

Piotrowski, Steve, *The Birds of Suffolk* (London:
Christopher Helm, 2003)

Richmond, W. Kenneth, 'The return of the Barnacle
Goose', *Country Life* (2 March 1961), pp. 450–1

Ritchie, Anna, *Picts* (Edinburgh: HMSO, 1990)

Scott, Peter, *The Eye of the Wind: An autobiography* (London: Hodder and Stoughton, 1961)

Scott, Peter, 'The wariest of fowl', *Country Life* (21 June 1930), pp. 910–12

Scott, Peter, 'Wild Geese: described and painted by Peter Scott', *Country Life* (24 August 1929), pp. 262–5

Scott, Peter and James Fisher, *A Thousand Geese* (London: Collins, 1953)

Scott, Sir Walter, *Redgauntlet* (Edinburgh: Adam & Charles Black, 1887)

Shrubb, Michael, *Feasting, Fowling and Feathers: A History of the Exploitation of Wild Birds* (London: T. & A. D. Poyser, 2013)

Stroud, David, Tony Fox, et al., *International Single Species Action Plan for the Conservation of the Greenland White-fronted Goose:* Anser albifrons flavirostris (Bonn: AEWA, 2012)

Wood, Simon, *The Birds of Essex* (London: Christopher Helm, 2007)

Internet resources

http://daunen.vier-pfoten.org/animal-welfare-issues/

Bibliography

http://www.essexfieldclub.org.uk/portal/p/Geology+
Site+Account/s/The+Naze+Cliffs+SSSI/o/The+Naze
+Cliffs+SSSI

https://www.hawaiitribune-herald.com/2018/04/03/
hawaii-news/nene-population-nears-3000-statewide/

https://jagareforbundet.se/projekt-fjallgas/flyttvagen-for-
svenska-fjallgass/

http://jncc.defra.gov.uk/pdf/UKSPA/UKSPA-A6-26.pdf

https://link.springer.com/
referenceworkentry/10.1007/978-1-4419-0465-2_2208

https://wwf.fi/mediabank/10369.pdf

https://monitoring.wwt.org.uk/our-work/goose-swan-
monitoring-programme/species-accounts/european-
white-fronted-goose/

https://monitoring.wwt.org.uk/our-work/goose-swan-
monitoring-programme/species-accounts/greenland-
white-fronted-goose/

https://piskulka.net/reintro.php

https://www.ramsar.org/on-the-migration-of-water-
and-the-flow-of-birds-in-the-upper-solway-ramsar-
site-uk

https://www.sovon.nl/sites/default/files/doc/Rap_
2013-48_Lesser_White-fronted_Geese.pdf

https://theferret.scot/film-geese-shot-injured-islay/
https://www.theguardian.com/environment/2019/feb/
   22/conservation-body-issues-170000-wild-bird-kill-
   permits-in-five-years?CMP=Share_AndroidApp_
   Tweet&__twitter_impression=true

Notes

Introduction

1. J. A. Baker, *The Peregrine* (New York: New York Review of Books, 2005), p. 10.

Chapter 1: Pink-footed Geese

1. David Cabot, *Wildfowl* (London: Collins, 2009), p. 290.
2. Hugh S. Gladstone, *The Birds of Dumfriesshire* (London: Witherby & Co., 1910), p. 246.
3. R. W. Forrester, I. J. Andrews, et al., *The Birds of Scotland: Volume 1* (Aberlady: The Scottish Ornithologists' Club, 2007), p. 143.
4. Aldo Leopold, *A Sand County Almanac* (Oxford: Oxford University Press, 1968), p. 23.
5. Kane Brides, Carl Mitchell, et al., *Status and distribution of Icelandic-breeding geese: results of the 2017 international census* (Slimbridge: Wildfowl and Wetlands Trust, 2018), p. 3.

Chapter 2: Barnacle Geese

1. Peter Scott, *The Eye of the Wind: An Autobiography* (London: Hodder and Stoughton, 1961), p. 7.

2. Ibid., p. 3.

3. Ibid., p. 82.

4. Peter Scott, 'Wild Geese: described and painted by Peter Scott', *Country Life*, 24 August 1929, pp. 262–5.

5. Peter Scott, 'The wariest of fowl', *Country Life*, 21 June 1930, pp. 910–12.

6. W. Kenneth Richmond, 'The return of the Barnacle Goose', *Country Life*, 2 March 1961, pp. 450–1.

7. https://www.hawaiitribune-herald.com/2018/04/03/hawaii-news/nene-population-nears-3000-statewide/

8. Scott, *The Eye of the Wind*, p. 171.

9. https://www.theguardian.com/environment/2019/feb/22/conservation-body-issues-170000-wild-bird-kill-permits-in-five-years?CMP=Share_AndroidApp_Tweet&__twitter_impression=true

10. Steve Percival and Eric Bignal, 'The Islay barnacle goose management strategy: A suggested way forward', *British Wildlife*, October 2018, p. 37.

11. Percival and Bignal, p. 39.

12. https://theferret.scot/film-geese-shot-injured-islay/

13. Aldo Leopold, *Round River: From the Journals of Aldo Leopold* (Oxford: Oxford University Press, 1993), pp. 169–70.

14. Ibid., p. 170.

15. Gladstone, *The Birds of Dumfriesshire*, p. 250.

16. Gerald of Wales, *The History and Topography of Ireland*, translated by John O'Meara (London: Penguin, 1982), p. 41.

17. Sir Ray Lankester, *Diversions of a Naturalist* (London: Methuen & Co., 1915), p. 119.

18. James Fisher and Peter Scott, *A Thousand Geese* (London: Collins, 1953), p. 11.

19. https://www.ramsar.org/on-the-migration-of-water-and-the-flow-of-birds-in-the-upper-solway-ramsar-site-uk

20. Sir Walter Scott, *Redgauntlet* (Edinburgh: Adam & Charles Black, 1887), p. 36.

21. Tim Birkhead, et al., *Ten Thousand Birds: Ornithology since Darwin* (Princeton: Princeton University Press, 2014), p. 402.

22. Steve Piotrowski, *The Birds of Suffolk* (London: Christopher Helm, 2003), p. 89.

Chapter 3: Greylag Geese

1. Michael Shrubb, *Feasting, Fowling and Feathers: A History of the Exploitation of Wild Birds* (London: T. and A. D. Poyser, 2013), p. 71.

2. Ibid., p. 17.

3. Kristiina Mannermaa, 'Goose: Domestication', in Claire Smith (ed.), *Encyclopedia of Global Archaeology* (New York: Springer, 2014); https://link.springer.com/referenceworkentry/10.1007/978-1-4419-0465-2_2208

4. Shrubb, p. 22.

5. Jeremy Mynott, *Birdscapes: Birds in Our Imagination and Experiences* (Princeton: Princeton University Press, 2009), p. 51.

6. Daniel Defoe, *A Tour Through the Whole Island of Great Britain* (London: Penguin, 1976), pp. 83–4.

7. Simon Wood, *The Birds of Essex* (London: Christopher Helm, 2007), p. 83.

8. Cabot, *Wildfowl*, p. 24.

9. Shrubb, p. 27.

10. Cabot, p. 25.

11. http://daunen.vier-pfoten.org/animal-welfare-issues/

12. Quoted in Jeremy Mynott, *Birds in the Ancient World* (Oxford: Oxford University Press, 2018), p. 179.

13. Edward A. Armstrong, *The Folklore of Birds* (London: Collins, 1958), p. 35.

Chapter 4: Brent Geese

1. Teresa Frost, et al., 'Population estimates of wintering water-birds in Great Britain', *British Birds*, vol. 112 (March 2019), p. 136.

2. http://www.essexfieldclub.org.uk/portal/p/Geology+Site+Account/s/The+Naze+Cliffs+SSSI/o/The+Naze+Cliffs+SSSI

3. Robin Hull, *Scottish Birds: Culture and Tradition* (Edinburgh: Mercat Press, 2001), p. 110.

4. http://jncc.defra.gov.uk/pdf/UKSPA/UKSPA-A6-26.pdf.

Chapter 5: White-fronted Geese

1. Scott, *The Eye of the Wind*, p. 574.

2. David Stroud, Tony Fox, et al., *International Single Species Action Plan for the Conservation of the Greenland White-fronted Goose:* Anser albifrons flavirostris (Bonn: AEWA, 2012), p. 22.

3. Ibid, p. 11.

4. Stroud, et al., p. 16.

5. Birkhead, et al., *Ten Thousand Birds*, p. 402.

6. https://monitoring.wwt.org.uk/our-work/goose-swan-monitoring-programme/species-accounts/european-white-fronted-goose/

7. Frost, et al., p. 136.

8. Cabot, *Wildfowl*, p. 73.

9. https://monitoring.wwt.org.uk/our-work/goose-swan-monitoring-programme/species-accounts/greenland-white-fronted-goose/

10. Stroud, et al., p. 16.

11. Ibid.

12. Ibid., p. 24.

13. Axel Hirschfeld, Geraldine Attard, et al., 'Bird hunting in Europe: an analysis of bag figures and the potential impact on the conservation of threatened species', *British Birds*, vol. 112 (March 2019), p. 160.

14. Scott, *The Eye of the Wind*, p. 547.

15. Cabot, p. 81.

16. https://www.sovon.nl/sites/default/files/doc/Rap_2013-48_Lesser_White-fronted_Geese.pdf

17. Fennoscandian lesser white-fronted goose project, https://piskulka.net/reintro.php

18. Ibid.

19. John H. Marchant and Andrew J. Musgrove, 'Review of European flyways of the Lesser White-fronted Goose *Anser erythropus*', Research Report 595 (Thetford: British Trust for Ornithology, 2011), p. 14.

20. https://jagareforbundet.se/projekt-fjallgas/flyttvagen-for-svenska-fjallgass/

21. Richard Attenborrow, 'Lesser white-fronted goose – revisited', *Harrier*, no. 195 (Winter 2018), p. 11

22. John Grant, 'A wild goose chase with a difference', *Harrier*, no. 180 (Spring 2015), p. 8.

Chapter 6: Bean Geese

1. Cabot, *Wildfowl*, p. 63.

2. Mark Cocker and Richard Mabey, *Birds Britannica* (London: Chatto & Windus, 2005), p. 69.
3. Cocker, et al., p. 69.
4. Baker, *The Peregrine*, p. 12.
5. Forrester, et al., *Birds of Scotland*, pp. 138–40.
6. https://www.poemhunter.com/poem/a-winter-day-morning/
7. Forrester, et al., *Birds of Scotland*, pp. 138–40.

Index

Index

Index

Index

ABOUT THE AUTHOR

Stephen Rutt is an award-winning writer, birder, naturalist, and book reviewer whose work has appeared in *EarthLines Magazine*, *Zoomorphic*, *The Harrier*, *Surfbirds*, *BirdGuides* and the *East Anglian Times*. He is the recipient of the Roger Deakin Award from the Society of Authors for *The Seafarers*, his first book, which won the Saltire First Book of the Year in 2019. Stephen currently lives in Dumfries.

Also by Stephen Rutt

The British Isles are remarkable for their extraordinary seabird life: spectacular gatherings of charismatic Arctic terns, elegant fulmars and stoic eiders, to name a few.

In *The Seafarers*, Stephen Rutt escapes his hectic life in London to journey around the most remote and dramatic reaches of our shores. There he explores the landscapes shaped not by us but by the birds, revealing the allure of a remote and wild landscape in an over-crowded world.

ISBN: 978-1-78396-504-5 | RRP: £9.99